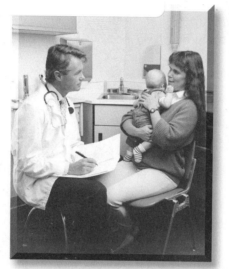

Health Insurance

The Silver Lake Editors

Made E-Z

MADE E-Z PRODUCTS™
Deerfield Beach, Florida / www.Mad

Health Insurance Made E-Z™
The Silver Lake Editors
Silver Lake Publishing
2025 Hyperion Avenue
Los Angeles, California 90027
www.silverlakepub.com

Table of Contents

Introduction

If you've ever been sick or injured, you know that it's important to have the right kind of health insurance. It pays for the pain to be abated and the damage to be repaired. But, if your employer offers you a choice of health plans, do you have enough knowledge to make the right choice? In addition to medical expense coverage, do you need any other kind of insurance? What will happen if you are too sick to work? Or, if you are over 65, will Medicare pay for all your health care expenses? If you're confused about the types of health coverage available and what coverage is best for you, your family and even your business, you're not alone.

Today's consumers are asking these same questions, and the questions aren't always easy to answer. Many of the insurance agents and brokers who used to explain the details to people are gone. Companies that sell medical insurance rely on a shrinking number of experts to explain coverages to people—and most of these experts focus their pitch on the start of a new plan with a client. If questions come up later—which is usually the case—people often get some brochures and a shrug of the shoulders.

Tips for smart shoppers always sound a little bit like basic common sense. Be wary of a plan whose description of benefits sounds too good to be true. It may be. Often, agents—in an attempt to convince you to purchase a policy from them—will give inaccurate, exaggerated, and misleading descriptions of the benefits provided by policies.

Similarly, agents sometimes try to get you to surrender insurance you already own and replace your coverage with a policy they are selling by misrepresenting the policy, by making an incomplete comparison of the policies, or even by telling you that your current company is in financial trouble.

You can even check out the insurance companies' financial stability ratings. A.M. Best Co. rates each company on a letter scale from A to F, in order to provide an overall indication of the company's ability to meet its policyholder obligations. Their ratings are based on financial strength, the company's market profile and operating performance. For instance, A++ and A+ indicate Superior while F indicates the company is in liquidation. These ratings can be found at your local library or online.

As with all insurance policies, it pays to compare the costs of similar policies available from different insurers. Shop aggressively when you first buy a policy. After that, change insurers or policies only when you desire to make substantial changes to your coverage. If you cancel one policy to purchase another, there is generally no refund of premium, and you may be subject to new policy limitations and restrictions.

In short, there is a plan to meet your needs. Remember to review the cost, check the benefits and the service issues that are important to you, before you make a choice. And, don't be afraid to ask questions.

Health Insurance Basics

1

Health Insurance Basics

Making Sense of Health Insurance

Health coverage refers to a collection of insurance policies and government programs which pay for a range of costs—from doctors and hospitals to more specific needs, such as long-term care expenses or disability insurance (which replaces lost income if you can't work because of an illness or accident).

Health insurance doesn't just cover medical expenses. It may provide payment of benefits for the loss of income and/or the medical expenses arising from illness or injury. Therefore, health insurance is sometimes called other things, like accident and sickness insurance or accident and health insurance. The different kinds of health insurance coverages vary according to the methods of underwriting, the injury or illness covered, types of insurers, types of benefits and services provided, types of losses covered, and the amount of benefits available.

When people refer to *health insurance*, they usually mean group insurance offered by employers—insurance that covers such things as medical bills, surgery, and hospital expenses. Insurance companies call this comprehensive or major medical coverage because of the broad protection it offers.

When health insurance first appeared in the United States—in the mid-1800s—it was sold by casualty insurance companies on a stand-alone basis and as an add-on to life insurance policies. Early policies covered losses due to accidental injuries. Later ones provided benefits due to illness as well as accidents.

Most consumers are familiar with some of these. The terms fee-for-service and managed care appear just about everywhere. The

> Today, health coverage includes insurance policies and government-provided benefits.

specific kinds of managed care plans—health maintenance organizations (HMOs), preferred provider organizations (PPOs), and point-of-service (POS) plans—are also fairly common. But what do these terms mean?

Both fee-for-service and managed care plans cover an array of medical, surgical, and hospital expenses. Most offer some coverage for prescription drugs, and some even include coverage for dentists and other providers. But because there are differences that will make one or another plan right for you, it is important to understand each kind of plan.

Fee-for-service Plans

Fee-for-service coverage generally assumes that a medical provider (usually a doctor or hospital) will be paid a fee for services rendered. The term refers to the way doctors are paid regardless of who pays. Paying cash—that is, unreimbursed out-of-pocket expenses—for medical treatment is a fee-for-service arrangement. However, most people don't pay cash for their medical care. Traditional health insurance—what insurance companies call *indemnity coverage*—is a fee-for-service arrangement.

With fee-for-service insurance, you choose the doctor you want to see, and you can choose a different doctor for any reason any time you feel like it. After you've been treated, you or your doctor submits a claim to your insurance company for reimbursement. You will only receive reimbursement for the covered medical expenses that are listed in your plan. For a sample list of covered expenses and/or examples of non-covered expenses, turn to Chapter 3.

With some variation, fee-for-service policies reimburse bills for a percentage of a reasonable service charge. (This amount is derived by the prevailing cost of a service in a geographic area.) The portion of the covered medical expenses that you pay, the other 20 percent, is called *co-insurance*. Sometimes a doctor will charge more than a reasonable amount for a service. If this is the case, you'll end up paying the difference out of your own pocket.

> Services that are covered under your policy are generally reimbursed for some—but not all—of the cost. Many policies pay 80 percent of the cost.

Example: If the reasonable charge for a service is $100, your insurer will probably pay $80 and you would pay $20. But if the doctor charged $105, you would have to pay $25. Many fee-for-service plans pay hospital expenses in full, so be sure to check with your plan provider.

Deductibles are the amount of the covered expenses that you must pay each year before your insurer will reimburse you. These can range from as little as $100 to $300 per year per person to $500 or more per family. Generally, the higher the deductible, the lower the premiums, which are the monthly, quarterly, or annual payments for the insurance.

Most policies have an out-of-pocket maximum—when your covered expenses reach a certain amount in a given calendar year, a reasonable fee for the benefits that are covered on your plan will be paid in full by your insurer and you no longer pay the co-insurance. However, if your doctor bills are more than the reasonable charge, you may still have to pick up some of the tab.

In addition to the out-of-pocket maximum, many policies place lifetime limits on benefits. When shopping for a plan, it's smart to look for a policy whose lifetime limit is at least $1 million. If the limit is much lower than this, you could run through the coverage if you had major health problems for several years.

Managed Care

Managed care plans provide comprehensive health services to their members and offer financial incentives for patients to use providers under contract with the plan. That's how managed care plans keep their costs low. (In recent years, though, even this tactic has had a diminishing effect.) Instead of paying for each service that you receive separately, the plans pay providers in advance. That's why insurance professionals call these plans prepaid care.

HMOs have been in existence for many years. However, their popularity has increased dramatically since the passage of the Health Maintenance Organization Act by the federal government in the late 1970s.

If you join an HMO, you'll pay a monthly or quarterly premium. That premium will remain the same—whatever your medical history and whether or not you use the plan's services. The plan will also charge a co-payment for certain services. For example: $10 for an office visit or $5 for a prescription. This is one of the ways in which the plans adjust for people who use the services more heavily than others.

By joining an HMO, you may have only a few out-of-pocket expenses for medical care—as long as you use doctors or hospitals that participate, or are part of, the HMO. HMOs generally don't require you to pay deductibles or co-insurance.

HMOs deliver care directly to patients. Whether patients go to a medical facility to see a doctor or to a specific doctor's office, their business relationship is with the HMO. To many people, the health care providers appear to be interchangeable subcontractors.

This appearance isn't exactly accurate. If you belong to an HMO, you usually have to receive your medical care through the plan by selecting a primary care physician who coordinates your care. A primary care physician may be a family practice doctor, an internist, a pediatrician, etc. He or she is responsible for referring you to specialists.

While most of these specialists will be participating providers in the HMO, there are circumstances in which patients enrolled in an HMO may be referred to providers outside the HMO network and still receive coverage. (However, this issue is a major controversy in HMOs. We'll consider the matter in greater detail in Chapter 5.)

Preferred provider organizations and point-of-service plans are the other major types of managed care. These plans combine the features of fee-for-service plans and HMOs. These plans provide choice regarding physician, hospital, etc. An HMO restricts choice to a network provider.

> PPOs and POSs generally offer more flexibility than HMOs, but their premiums tend to be somewhat higher.

With a PPO or a POS, unlike most HMOs, you will get some reimbursement if you receive a covered service from a provider who is not in the plan. Of course, choosing a provider outside the plan's network will cost you more than choosing a provider in the network. These plans will act like fee-for-service plans and charge you co-insurance when you go outside the network.

What is the difference between a PPO and a POS plan? A POS plan has primary care physicians who coordinate patient care, and in most cases, PPO plans do not.

In many cases, a PPO is under contract to—or a subsidiary of—a commercial insurer. Under such a program, the overall plan benefits may include preventive health care, diagnostic services, physicians' services, inpatient and outpatient benefits, etc. These types of services and benefits are provided under the basic medical plan and/or the PPO option.

Commercial Insurers and Service Organizations

Many of the major life and health insurance companies market various forms of hospitalization coverage, including both group and individual policies. Your insurance company may issue one or more types of hospitalization insurance.

The structure of the commercial insurer offering hospitalization policies generally includes a marketing department, underwriting department, and a claims and administration section. These are organizations which provide prepaid medical and health benefits. The best example of this type of provider is Blue Cross/Blue Shield. This system began in 1939 as part of the California Physicians' Service. This early plan was designed to pay doctors' fees. The American Medical Association was closely involved with the early development of medical association service plans.

Most Blue Cross-Blue Shield plans are organized in accordance with state laws which recognize them as nonprofit service organizations and exempt them from state premium taxation. Depending on the state, Blue Cross-Blue Shield may or may not technically operate as an insurer. Regardless, they are regulated by the state insurance departments.

Normally, Blue Cross pays hospital expenses and Blue Shield covers physician charges.

Unlike a commercial insurer, which issues a policy and has a contractual relationship with the insured, service organizations have a contractual relationship with the providers of health care, namely doctors and hospitals. Subscribers to this health care service then use the services of the contracted doctors and hospitals commonly referred to as participating providers. All claims are settled directly with the providers by Blue Cross-Blue Shield.

Other Coverages

Various kinds of insurance—most tied to some form of life insurance or related coverages—can provide health coverage for people or groups who can't get the protection they want from standard policies.

We'll consider some of these coverages in greater detail later in this book. Here, we'll take a quick look at the important ones.

> Used on a stand-alone basis—or combined with each other—alternative coverages can work for people whose health or medical history makes traditional health insurance difficult

Accidental Death and Dismemberment (AD&D)

Although a health insurance product, AD&D benefits are frequently provided as riders—attachments to a policy that modify its conditions by expanding or restricting benefits—to individual and group life insurance contracts. AD&D benefits may be included as riders on life insurance policies, as part of disability income insurance, as part of health insurance, or as a separate policy.

AD&D coverage pays the policy's principal sum in accordance with policy provisions. A principal sum is similar to a policy's face amount. This same amount is paid if you suffer the actual severance of two arms, two legs, or the loss of vision in two eyes due to an accident. If the policy is paying an accidental dismemberment benefit, this amount is identified as the capital sum.

Medical Expense Benefits

Medical expense insurance, commonly referred to as hospitalization insurance, provides benefits for expenses incurred for hospital medical treatment/surgery as well as certain outpatient expenses like doctor's visits, lab tests and diagnostic services. The policy can be issued as an individual policy covering all family members or as a group insurance policy provided through an employer-sponsored program.

Dental expense benefits are generally sold as part of group hospitalization coverage. Dental benefits are provided for preventive maintenance (cleanings and x-rays), repair (fillings, root canals, etc.) and replacement of teeth.

> Most insurers do not provide individual dental coverage

Long-term care (LTC) insurance pays for the care of persons with chronic diseases or disabilities, and may include a wide range of health and social services provided under the supervision of medical professionals. LTC often covers nursing home care, home-based care and respite care.

Limited Health Exposures and Long-term Contracts

There are a variety of special health insurance policies providing limited coverage. To ensure that you have sufficient notice that your coverage is limited, your policy, by law, should state plainly that it is a limited policy.

Travel accident insurance provides coverage for death or injury resulting from accidents occurring while the insured is a fare-paying passenger on a common carrier.

Specified disease or dread disease insurance provides a variety of benefits for only certain diseases, usually cancer or heart disease. This coverage is especially important for people with a history of a particular illness—because this is how they can insure against other problems. For example, a person who has survived cancer may have trouble finding standard health coverage but may be able to get coverage for heart trouble.

Hospital income insurance pays a specified sum on a daily, weekly or monthly basis while the insured is confined to a hospital. The amount of the benefit is not related to expenses incurred or to wages lost while the insured is hospitalized.

Accident only insurance provides coverage for injury from accident—but excludes sickness. Benefits may be paid for all or any of the following: death, disability, dismemberment or hospital expenses.

Blanket insurance is a form of group coverage. Often the individual's name is not known because the individuals come and go. These groups include students, campers, passengers of a common carrier, volunteer groups, and sports teams. Unlike group insurance the individuals are automatically covered under the blanket policy, and they do not receive certificates of insurance.

Prescription Coverage

Prescription medication coverage is normally provided as an optional benefit under a group medical expense policy. The insured and eligible dependents are provided with a stated cost for any prescription medication required. This specific cost is usually, two, three, or five dollars per prescription. Thus, regardless of the cost of the medication, the insured only pays the stated amount, and the balance of the prescription cost is paid by the insurance company.

Medicare and Government Plans

Medicare is health insurance for the aged or disabled. *Aged* means 65 years old or older. (Though Congress has recently considered raising the qualifying age to 67.) *Disabled* means that the person is totally disabled as determined by Social Security or an individual has a major kidney problem which requires dialysis treatment. Reaching age 65 or having disability status qualifies an individual for this federal health care program.

Medicare is financed through the payment of the Medicare tax which is part of the total Social Security taxes paid by workers and their employers.

The other main federal health care program is Medicaid. Like Medicare, this coverage has many limitations.

In addition to state and federal programs in which the government becomes a health care provider, there are other organizations and entities which serve as health care providers.

> Qualification for benefits under Medicaid is based on financial need. And, even then, the coverage is limited. It's not great coverage.

We will consider these programs (including Medicare and Medicaid) in greater length later in this book.

How Do You Get Your Health Insurance?

Now that you have a working knowledge of the types of plans out there, you probably want to know how to purchase this coverage.

Health insurance is generally available on an individual or group basis. Premiums tend to be lower for group coverage—and this is how most people get their health insurance.

Group coverage is typically offered through your employer, but unions, professional associations, and other organizations also offer this type of insurance.

When you receive group insurance at work, the premium usually is paid through your employer. In some cases, the employer pays some or all of this premium as an additional benefit. In others, the premium will be deducted from your pay.

Group coverage has distinct advantages. Most of the costs may be borne by your employer. Premiums are lower due to lower administration costs for large groups. Eligibility for group coverage is usually open when you start a job—you won't have to undergo a physical exam to prove you're insurable.

Know your choices. Some employers offer employees a choice of fee-for-service and managed care plans. In addition, some group plans offer dental insurance as well as medical.

Individual insurance is a main option if you are self-employed or work for a small company that doesn't offer health insurance. Mechanically, an individual policy works in the same way that a group policy does—the main difference is that the premiums are usually higher because the administrative costs are, too.

One advantage of individual insurance: You can tailor a plan to fit your needs. However, shop carefully. Coverage and costs vary widely, so be sure to evaluate the medical services covered, benefits paid, and what you must pay in deductibles and co-insurance—for each kind of coverage.

Self-funded plans

Your employer may have set up a financial arrangement that helps cover employees' health care expenses. Sometimes employers do this and have the health plan administered by an insurance company, but sometimes there is no outside administrator.

A self-funded plan is a program which allows a financially secure employer to assume the risk for health care costs instead of transferring the risk to an insurance company. The employer's funds are used to pay benefits directly to the employees. Instead of paying insurance policy premiums to an insurer, the employer places a sum of money into a secured account to provide health care benefits, usually with certain limitations. In essence, the employer has become a "mini-insurer" providing various types or levels of health care.

A self-insured plan is a less expensive way for an employer to provide health care benefits, provided the claims experience is favorable and the employer can realize a good rate of return on the money deposited in the trust account. Employers often choose a self-funded plan to cover their employees' dental expenses because it is less expensive than purchasing a dental plan.

With a self-funded plan an employer, not an insurance company, provides the funds to pay claims for company employees and their dependents. In the event that claims are higher than predicted, a self-funded health insurance plan can be backed-up by a stop-loss contract. A stop-loss contract is designed to limit the employer's liability for claims.

There are two variations of this coverage. Specific stop-loss coverage begins to apply after an individual's medical expenses exceed a predetermined amount—such as $5,000. Aggregate stop-loss coverage applies when the employer's liability for group insurance claims exceeds a specified amount. The insurance company pays all claims once the specified amount is reached.

A self-funded plan may be an indemnity program which reimburses covered employees for medical care they have received. Or, the employer may provide benefits through the service plan offered under an HMO, or through a company's PPO network.

An insurance company can also be used by a self-funded employer under an "administrative services only" (ASO) contract. Under an ASO agreement the insurance company provides claim

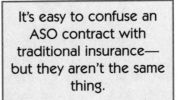

It's easy to confuse an ASO contract with traditional insurance— but they aren't the same thing.

forms, administers claims and makes payments to providers, but the employer still provides the funds to make payments.

What Is Not Covered

While HMO benefits are generally more comprehensive than those of traditional fee-for-service plans, no health plan will cover every medical expense. Most plans won't cover eyeglasses or hearing aids because these are considered budgetable expenses. Very few cover elective cosmetic surgery, except to correct damage caused by a covered accidental injury. Some fee-for-service plans won't cover checkups. And some plans cover complications arising from pregnancy but not normal pregnancy or childbirth.

You should also remember that insurers will not pay duplicate benefits. You and your spouse may each be covered under a health insurance plan at work but, under what is called a coordination of benefits provision, the total you can receive under both plans for a covered medical expense cannot exceed 100 percent of the allowable cost. Also note that if neither of your plans covers 100 percent of your expenses you will only be covered for the percentage of coverage (for example, 80 percent) that your primary plan covers. This provision benefits everyone in the long run because it helps to keep costs down.

> Fee-for-service plans generally won't cover experimental procedures.

Preexisting Conditions

If you or a family member covered under your policy has a preexisting condition you won't have to worry about whether or not your coverage will transfer when you change jobs thanks to a recent change in federal law. As of July 1997, insurance companies can impose only one 12-month waiting period for any preexisting condition treated or diagnosed in the previous six months. As long as you have maintained coverage without a break for more than 62 days, your prior health insurance coverage will be credited toward the preexisting condition exclusion period. Pregnancy won't apply here, but the 12-month waiting period is waived for any newborns or adopted children who are covered within 30 days. If you've had group coverage for two years, switch jobs and move to another plan, the new health plan can't impose another preexisting condition exclusion period.

Federal law also makes it easier for you to get individual insurance under certain situations. If you aren't covered under a group plan and can't get insurance on your own, check with your state insurance department to see if it has a risk pool. Like risk pools for automobile insurance, these can provide health insurance if you can't get it elsewhere. But they can get expensive.

Summary

The information economy is tearing down traditional notions of companies and employer/employee relations. This is having a major impact on how people get health insurance. At the same time, large parts of the insurance industry—especially those dealing with life and car insurance—are dealing directly with consumers. Whether by mail, telephone or Internet, the big companies are cutting out the middlemen.

However, these middlemen—insurance agents—provide important information and advice to consumers. As their numbers decline, a growing number of people will be left without the tools to make good decisions.

This book will give you those tools. It may not answer all your questions, but it will give you the concepts and language to ask the right questions of the right person.

Key Terms and Definitions

2

Key Terms and Definitions

Obviously, understanding the jargon of any field is essential to mastering the business done there. In this chapter—before moving on to detailed discussions of specific health coverages—we will review some of the key terms and definitions.

Accidental

In a health insurance policy, *accidental* means unexpected or an undesigned cause of bodily injury. A related term—*accidental means*—the mishap itself must be accidental not just the resulting injury. An example: You are chopping wood when the ax slips from your hand and cuts your foot. This is accidental means. However, if your finger gets in the way of the ax, it may not count as accidental means.

Accidental Death and Dismemberment

AD&D coverage is a policy or a provision of a policy that pays either a specific amount or a multiple of a weekly disability benefit. The full coverage takes effect if the policyholder loses his or her sight—or two limbs—in an accident. (A lower amount is payable if the person loses one eye or one limb.)

Acute Care

Acute Care means skilled, medically necessary care provided by medical and nursing professionals in order to restore the person to health or the ability to function. For example, acute care would be rendered to persons recovering from major surgery.

Additional Insured

A person other than the named insured who is protected under the terms of a policy. Usually, *additional insureds* are added by endorsement or are described in the definition of insured in the policy.

Age Change

The date on which a person's age—for insurance purposes—changes is an important coverage point. In most policies, health insurers use the age at the previous birthday for rate determinations.

Assisted Living Facility

Assisted Living Facility means a senior residential community which makes custodial and nursing care available to residents who need it, while allowing them to live in a home-like setting.

Basic Premium

This is a fixed cost charged in a retrospective rating plan. The basic plan is a kind of starting point—a percentage of the standard premium, designed to give the insurance company enough money to cover administrative expenses and commissions.

Benefit Period

The *benefit period* defines the period during which you are eligible for benefits. Usually, a 90-day benefit

> There is no limit to the number of 90-day benefit periods you can have.

period starts with each illness and commences the day

you are admitted to a hospital and ends when you have not been hospitalized for a period of 60 consecutive days.

Capitation

Capitation (CAP) is the fixed amount of money paid on a monthly basis to an HMO medical group or to an individual health provider for the full medical care of an individual.

Case Management

Case Management means the assessment of a person's LTC needs and the appropriate recommendations for care, monitoring and follow-up as to the extent and quality of the services provided.

Case Manager

A *case manager* is a health professional (e.g. nurse, doctor, social worker) affiliated with a health plan who is responsible for coordinating and approving the medical care of an individual enrolled in a managed care plan.

Closed panel

This is a system in which insured people must select one primary care physician who will refer patients to other health care providers within the plan. This is also called a *closed access* or *gatekeeper system*.

Co-insurance

Co-insurance is the percentage of your medical bills that you are expected to pay. Co-insurance payments usually constitute a fixed percentage of the total cost of a medical service covered by the plan. If a health plan pays 80 percent of a physician's bill, the remaining 20 percent which the member pays is referred to as co-insurance.

Co-payment

A *co-payment* is the fee paid by a plan member for medical services. A co-payment would be the out-of-pocket expenses you are expected to pay, such as $10 for an office visit or $5 for a prescription.

Covered Expenses

Health care expenses incurred by an insured person that qualify for reimbursement under the terms of a policy are, simply, *covered expenses*. This is an easy concept to describe in the abstract—but it can become quite complicated in a dispute.

Deductible

The sum of money that an individual must pay out of pocket for medical expenses before a

> Deductibles for family coverage often range from $200 to $500 per year.

health plan reimburses a percentage of additional covered medical expenses is called the *deductible*.

Elimination Period

Elimination Period (EP) means the period of time, usually expressed in days or months, at the beginning of a confinement in a long-term care facility, during which no benefits are payable. The EP could be defined as a "time deductible."

Fee-For-Service

Health insurance plans which reimburse physicians and hospitals for each individual service they provide are called *fee-for-service* plans. These plans allow insureds to chose any physician or hospital.

Formulary

This is a health plan's list of approved prescription medications for which it will reimburse members or pay for directly. Additional medications are usually not available to plan members.

Gatekeeper Physician

The primary care physician who directs the medical care of HMO members is the *gatekeeper physician*. The primary care physician determines if patients should be referred for specialty care.

Health Care Financing Administration

The *Health Care Financing Administration* (HCFA), part of the Department of Health and Human Services, administers Medicare and Medicaid with the assistance of Social Security Administration offices throughout the country. The HCFA establishes standards for medical providers and organizations if they are to satisfy the requirements to be certified as a qualified Medicare provider.

Health Maintenance Organizations (HMOs)

These are health plans that contract with medical groups to provide a full range of health services for their enrollees for a fixed pre-paid, per-member fee. There are three different kind of HMOs:

- Group model HMOs contract with independent groups of physicians that provide coordinated care for large numbers of HMO patients for a fixed, per-member fee. These groups will often care for the members of several HMOs.

- Staff model HMOs employ salaried physicians and other health professionals who provide care solely for members of one HMO.

- Independent practice associations (IPA) contract with groups of independent physicians who work in their own offices. These independent practitioners receive a per-member payment or capitation from the HMO to provide a full range of health services for HMO members. These providers often care for members of many HMOs.

A growing number of HMOs now offer a Point of Service (POS) option. These "escape hatch" plans allow HMO members to seek care from non-HMO physicians, but the premiums for POS plans are more costly than those for traditional HMOs. Moreover, when an HMO member receives care from a non-participating physician or hospital, the HMO pays far less than its usual 100 percent coverage of necessary medical services.

Health Insurance Plan

This term includes an HMO, preferred provider organization or traditional health insurance plan that covers a set range of health services.

Home Health Care

Home Health Care is care received at the patient's home, such as part-time skilled nursing care, speech, physical or occupational therapy, or part-time services of home health aides.

Hospice Care

Hospice Care refers to nursing services provided to the terminally ill. It's offered in a hospice, a nursing home, or in the patient's home where nurses and social workers can visit on a regular basis. The purpose of the care is to keep the patient comfortable and to enable the patient to die with dignity.

Indemnity Contracts

Indemnity Contracts are policies which provide a daily benefit, such as $50, $60, $70 per day, for each day of confinement in a hospital or long-term care facility. This method of payment can be contrasted with an expense incurred contract which reimburses for actual expenses incurred while confined.

Intermediate Nursing Care

Medically supervised health care and services for individuals who do not require the level of care and supervision provided by hospitals or nursing homes is called *Intermediate Nursing Care*. Typically, the degree of care provided is between acute and custodial care.

Intermediary

An *intermediary* is a private insurance company contracted by the Department of Health and Human Services for the purpose of processing payments to patients and health care providers.

Limited Health Insurance

These special health insurance policies provide limited coverage for specific injuries or illnesses such as travel accidents, particular diseases and hospital income.

Long-Term Care

Long-Term Care (LTC) is care which is provided for persons with chronic disease or disabilities. The term includes a wide range of health and social services which may involve adult day care, custodial care, home health care, hospice care, intermediate care, respite care and skilled nursing care. LTC does not include hospital care.

Managed Care

Managed Care refers to a broad and constantly changing array of health plans which attempt to control the cost and quality of care by coordinating medical and other health-related services. The vast majority of Americans with private health insurance are currently enrolled in managed care plans.

Proposals currently being considered by the United States Congress would, if enacted, guarantee that many millions of Americans who are covered by Medicare and Medicaid will soon join managed health care plans.

Medicaid

Medicaid is the federal-state health insurance program for low income Americans. Medicaid also foots the bill for nursing-home care for the indigent elderly and mentally disabled.

Medicare

Medicare is a federal health insurance program for persons age 65 or older, individuals with permanent kidney failure and certain persons who are totally disabled. The program was implemented in 1965 as part of the amendments to the Social Security Act of 1935.

Hospital Insurance of Medicare provides for inpatient hospital care, skilled nursing home care, home health care and hospice care. Part A of Medicare is automatically made available to persons age 65 who have been covered under Social Security.

Medical Insurance of Medicare is a voluntary program which covers physician's services, physical therapy, ambulance expenses, medical equipment and generally, out-patient services. A premium is charged to the individual when Part B coverage is elected.

Nursing Home Care

Nursing Home Care includes nursing and custodial care provided in a nursing home setting.

Peer Review

Groups of doctors who are paid by the federal government to conduct pre-admission, continued stay, and reviews of services provided to Medicare patients by Medicare approved hospitals are referred to as *peer review organizations* (PROs).

Preventive Care

An approach to health care which emphasizes preventive measures such as routine physical exams, diagnostic tests (e.g. PAP tests), immunization, etc.

Preferred Provider Organization

A health plan that encourages savings by establishing a network of preferred providers—health professionals who agree to provide medical services to plan members for discounted rates. Plan members may go "out of network" to seek medical services from non-affiliated medical professionals. Members are charged higher co-payments for this option.

Primary Care Physician

HMOs require that members be assigned to a primary care physician who functions as a gatekeeper.

Primary Care Physicians provide basic health services to their patients. General practitioners, pediatricians, family practice physicians and internists are recognized by health plans as primary care physicians.

Prospective Payment

A system of Medicare reimbursement which bases most hospital payments on the patient's diagnosis at the time of hospital admission rather than the costs the hospital actually incurs prior to discharging the patient is called a *prospective payment* system.

Respite Care

Normally associated with hospice care, respite care is for the family of the patient. The patient may be admitted to a nursing home or hospice for care. This care constitutes a respite—or break—for family members taking primary care of the patient.

Risk Contract

This is an arrangement through which a health provider agrees to provide a range of medical services to a population of patients for a pre-paid sum of money. The physician is responsible for managing the care of these patients and risks losing money if expenses exceed the pre-determined amount.

Skilled Nursing Care

Skilled Nursing Care is daily nursing and rehabilitative care that is performed only by, or under the supervision of, skilled professional or technical personnel. The care is based on a physician's orders and performed directly by or under the supervision of a registered nurse. This care would include administering prescription drugs, medical diagnosis, minor surgery, etc.

A *Skilled Nursing Facility* is a facility, licensed by the state, which provides 24-hour-a-day nursing services under the supervision of a physician or registered nurse.

Utilization Review

This includes the various methods used by health plans to measure the amount and appropriateness of health services used by its members. These checks can occur before, during, and after services have been sought or received from health professionals.

Summary

These are a few of the basic definitions and terms that apply to insuring your health. You will see these definitions—and others—throughout the book. Where needed, we will reiterate and expand definitions to provide you with the tools necessary to understand the language of health care financing.

Indemnity
Insurance

Indemnity Insurance

The rising cost of health care over the past 25 years—largely shouldered by business—has driven the problems in the health care system. Until the early 1980s, most people received health coverage through a traditional indemnity or fee-for-service plan. Under this type of plan, your insurance company pays all or part of the bill for any doctor, hospital or other health care provider that you may choose.

With traditional insurance, also called indemnity insurance, you are free to visit the doctor of your choice. You can change to another doctor at any time for any reason. And you can use any hospital or licensed medical facility you choose.

Indemnity plans existed before the rise of HMOs, PPOs and other types of managed care plans. However, indemnity plans—with their focus on flexibility—aren't very effective at controlling costs. In the early 1990s, indemnity plans lost their leading position in the U.S. health coverage market. Starting in 1993 or 1994 (depending on which survey you believe) more Americans got their health coverage through managed care plans.

Still, indemnity plans are the standard by which American health care plans are measured. They remain the main alternative to managed care systems, even though they're mostly the choice of larger corporations and wealthier individuals.

The conventional wisdom—within the medical profession and among consumers—is that people with traditional indemnity insurance get better treatment. And, most importantly, the traditional plans give policyholders the assurance that any decisions a health care provider makes are squarely in the patient's best interest. But, we we will see in this chapter, these distinctions are not as clear-cut as some people like to think.

What "Indemnity" Means

When insurance people talk about indemnity insurance, the thing that's being indemnified is "you, the policyholder." An indemnity insurance contract states that the insurance company will pay your medical bills. In some cases, it will reimburse the insured person for bills paid out-of-pocket. In other cases, it will pay bills directly to the doctor or hospital providing services. In either case, it pays fees for medical services after they are provided. This structure puts most of the decisions about health care and treatment on the shoulders of the policyholders, who usually defer to the suggestions that their doctors make.

With the service provider (the doctor) strongly influencing the decisions about how much and what kind of service should be provided, at least one truth emerges about indemnity coverage: It's not very effective for containing costs.

Because indemnity coverage was just about the only kind of health insurance around in the United States during the first three-quarters of the twentieth century, doctors and hospitals made a lot of money for a long time.

Conceptually, the coverage is pretty simple. In practice, it comes with some qualifiers. Insurance companies recognized pretty quickly that orthopedists in Miami and ob/gyns in Seattle were driving Mercedes, building second houses and sending their kids to Harvard—often at the same time. So, the companies started to put limits on how much an indemnification contract would indemnify.

The first limit is the deductible. The deductible works this way: The insurance company will pay the doctor and hospital bills after you pay a small amount first. This small fee is defined at the start of the policy period, and it's usually structured to spread over the whole period.

For example, the insurance company might indemnify you for all medical costs after the first $500 each year or the first $50 each month.

The point isn't so much to get you to pay part of the cost as it is to make sure you only go to the doctor when you're really sick.

Said another way: It's not that the insurance company needs you to pay the first $50 in medical bills each month. The company just figures that if you have to pay $50, you're less likely to go to the hospital with a low-grade fever. In health coverage, as in other kinds of insurance, these up-front fees are very effective at reducing bills generated by policyholders.

Another limit is co-insurance. This modification is an effort to get you to bear part of the cost. In a contract with a co-insurance clause, the insurance company agrees to pay a certain portion (80 percent is common) of the medical bills you incur. This shared burden applies from the first dollar of coverage to the policy's absolute limit. The rest—the other 20 percent—you have to pay out-of-pocket. This is a major compromise for the concept of full indemnification. Insurance companies usually make it financially appealing to take the lesser coverage.

It's easy to calculate how much the insurance company wants you to share the burden. Compare the annual premium for full indemnity coverage with the annual premium for indemnity coverage with an 80/20 co-insurance split. (Many companies will sell both kinds of insurance.) The full indemnity coverage should be about 25 percent more expensive. If it's that much more or less, the company doesn't mind the risk—and you should buy the full coverage. If it's more than 25 percent more—and most will be—you may be better off with the cheaper coverage.

A caveat: Many indemnity policies have both a deductible and a co-insurance clause. In these cases, you'll probably want to focus your negotiating efforts on lowering your portion of the co-insurance. The deductible doesn't usually impact the value of the policy as much.

Another limit is that some indemnity policies don't cover specifically-named medical services. These may not cover prescription drugs or routine doctor visits.

The final limit is the category of exclusions the indemnity contract includes. Many companies will agree to pay medical bills except for those related to a list of specific illnesses or conditions.

The best example of this: Many individual indemnity policies exclude coverage for pregnancy and childbirth. The companies look at this as an optional condition which has more complexities—and hidden costs—than most people realize.

Usual, Customary, and Reasonable Fees

Most of the limits and conditions we've considered so far merely trim at the edges of indemnity health coverage. There are bigger changes that have impacted—and usually limited— coverage.

Beginning in the 1970s, some indemnity insurance companies borrowed a few cost-saving tricks from the federal government's Medicare program and started using schedules of usual, customary and reasonable (UCR) fees that they would pay for specific kinds of medical treatments.

Approved providers (a group slightly less rigidly defined than network providers in a managed care plan) would agree to accept these fees as full payment for each service provided—within the policy's limits, of course.

This trend has caught on with indemnity companies to the point they are quite common. UCR fees don't get a lot of attention in the insurance industry—which is curious. They are a big reason that the distinctions between indemnity insurance and managed care are beginning to blur.

If your indemnity insurance company uses an UCR fee schedule—and if you don't use a participating provider—you may be responsible for the difference between the UCR fee and what the provider charges for a service. Even if you adhere to the UCR fee schedule, you'll also be subject to any deductibles and co-insurance requirements.

As you can see, taken together, these coverage limitations begin to erode the impression of blanket coverage that indemnity plans have for most people. They are the tools that even indemnity plans use for denying or only partially paying claims.

Traditional Insurance vs. Managed Care

If you want to share in the decision-making, greater flexibility and direct access to providers, you'll want to look into an indemnity plan. If you want lower premiums, managed care will usually work better.

Most people know this much about health insurance. But how do these two main versions of health coverage compare in a more detailed way? Here are some quick comparisons:

- **Choice**
  - ° **Indemnity Insurance:** You can select any doctor, hospital or other health care provider.
  - ° **Managed Care:** You can select any health care provider in the network. If you use a provider outside of the network, you pay some or all of the bill.

- **Seeing a specialist**
  - ° **Indemnity Insurance:** You can use any specialist. However, some plans require pre-approval for certain procedures performed by specialists.

- ° **Managed Care:** Your primary care doctor determines if and when you need to see a specialist. (Sometimes you can see a specialist who is part of the network without permission.) If you use a specialist without HMO approval (or outside the approved list), you will have to pay the entire bill.

- **Out-of-pocket costs**

  - ° **Indemnity Insurance:** You may have to pay an annual deductible of $200 to $1,000. You also may be responsible for co-insurance payments of something like 20 percent of your medical bills, up to a certain limit (the stop-loss amount) each year. Sometimes, you pay for routine doctor visits and prescription drugs.

  - ° **Managed Care:** You may have to pay co-payments (usually $3 to $10) for network doctor visits and prescription drugs. When you use a provider outside of the network, you may have to pay a deductible after which the plan will pay part of the total charges.

In short, an indemnity plan—even with its limitations—offers you the freedom of choice but usually requires you to pay more out-of-pocket expenses than you would with an HMO or PPO.

The indemnity plan may not cover you for any routine care—annual checkups and other preventative treatments—either.

Some of these preventative treatments include:

- blood tests
- prostate exams
- genetic trait tests
- hearing and sight loss
- electro-cardiogram (stress tests)
- mammograms
- CAT scans (if you have a history of problems)

In an age of heavily-touted preventive medicine, the fact that these treatments aren't covered may seem strange. Of course, you can get these services under an indemnity plan. You just have to be willing to absorb the related costs—at least large parts of them—by yourself.

Choosing a Doctor

An indemnity insurance plan will usually require you to choose a primary care physician, if only to give the company a recognizable name to use when reviewing medical bills.

This selection is much less critical than choosing a primary physician under a managed care plan. For one thing, you can choose any physician you wish and any health services to use. You can also change "your doctor" any time you want—you just have to let the insurance company know. (And, frankly, you don't even need to do that too scrupulously.)

The same rule applies to seeing specialists. An indemnity plan allows you to go to any specialist whenever you prefer to without having to get a referral from your primary care physician.

An indemnity plan puts no limit on doctor visits, aside from your own financial well-being. However, certain types of visits may not be covered under an indemnity plan (i.e., mental health). This means you will have to bear the brunt of the costs.

This is all different from managed care plans, in which you choose a primary care physician from a list of doctors that your health plan has contracted with to provide health services. With an HMO, your primary care physician is your primary contact for all health services. Instead of having a choice, primary care doctor coordinates the services—provided by specialists and others—that you will receive.

Prescriptions

If you have an indemnity plan, prescriptions may or may not be covered under your plan. If it is covered, you may have to pay the larger portion while your insurance company pays a smaller share for your medications. However, you will have the option to choose either the brand name or the generic drug.

Preventative Care

As we've noted, one major difference between an indemnity plan and a managed care plan is that under the first, there are typically no wellness educational programs.

Usually, when you have indemnity coverage, you seek care only when it is needed for a particular condition. And bills are paid only after the care is delivered.

Managed care plans stress prevention and offer programs to help people learn about their conditions. This applies to facilities as well as physicians. The indemnity plan lets you choose to go to any hospital you wish, but it doesn't let you choose any service from that hospital. If you submit bills from a hospital's wellness program, they will likely be denied.

During the 1970s and early 1980s, some indemnity insurance companies did pay for certain wellness programs affiliated with hospitals. They stopped doing this in the late 1980s and early 1990s. However, the pendulum seems to be swinging— as some indemnity plans are allowing preventative care claims again.

Disputing Decisions

Unlike HMOs (which usually have to respond within six months), traditional indemnity plans are not required to respond to your complaints within a set time frame or have provisions for a formal hearing or appeals process. But if you are not satisfied with your insurer's willingness to pay a claim, you can ask for a reconsideration of the decision.

If you have problems getting reimbursed, an indemnity plan allows you to choose your method of recourse, i.e., the court system or mediation. In addition, you have the option to appeal any decision by your insurance company to pay or deny a claim.

You can also file a complaint with your state's Department of Commerce (or equivalent agency), and you don't have to tell your insurance company first. You will have to fill out a complaint form and supply any information needed to support your position to the Department.

Department investigators will usually then contact your insurance company, and, if the problem cannot be resolved within about 10 days, they will investigate whether the insurance company followed the terms of your policy.

Summary

In today's business world, employers have come to rely on managed care at the expense of traditional indemnity insurance. In fact, many employers no longer offer traditional insurance indemnity at all.

But economic realities and employee preferences clearly show that, despite its dramatic growth, people want freedom to choose their doctors and hospitals, and the networks that include them.

While cost will be one of your biggest concerns in choosing a plan, quality should also be an important consideration.

> One of the advantages of the indemnity plan is that there are typically no limits to which providers you can use or how often you see them.

The concept behind an indemnity plan is to reduce your share of the costs as much as possible—without compromising the quality of the care you receive. Some insurance companies do this more aggressively than others.

Generally, you have to shell out more for this type of plan—in deductibles, co-payments, premiums and out of pocket expenses—but you have an unlimited amount of choices. So, if you don't have financial limitations holding you back and you want to be able to go to the doctor you want, when you want and wherever you want, you may want to look into an indemnity plan.

Under a fee-for-service type plan, you pay a deductible—a fixed amount that must be paid before your insurance company will start to pay—and all costs for services that your insurance company won't pay for.

To recount, what are the advantages of traditional indemnity insurance over an HMO?

- You can choose any doctor.
- You can go to virtually any hospital, anywhere in the country.
- You can continue seeing the same doctor you always have even if you change jobs or insurance companies.
- You have some assurance that your doctor's medical recommendations are being made in your best interest—and not the insurance company's.

Even if you choose an indemnity health coverage plan, you can't rest assured that everything will be covered. It's important to investigate and learn as much about the types of policies available, the companies offering insurance, the agent and the local company represented, what the policy will or will not pay for, and how you will be reimbursed for visits, prescriptions, etc.

Be sure to review your policy at least once a year. Today's health care system continues to change at a rapid pace, and you wouldn't want to be making up the difference yourself in order to meet these changing demands.

Major
Medical

4

Major Medical 4

Indemnity health insurance comes in several common variations. The variations are based on specific coverage limitations that change the traditional indemnity policy substantially—so that it becomes, for all purposes, a different kind of coverage.

The most common variation in indemnity health coverage is the major medical policy. This coverage focuses on hospitalization costs, rather than health care costs in general. And it uses deductibles and absolute dollar limits differently than traditional indemnity insurance.

Major medical can be sold on an individual and group basis— and is sold aggressively to both. It provides benefits up to a high limit for most types of medical expenses incurred, subject to a large deductible. The contract may contain limits on specific types of charges, like room and board, and a co-insurance clause. These policies usually pay covered expenses whether an individual is in or out of the hospital. Another name for this type of contract is a catastrophe policy.

Because it covers costs related to hospitalization and has high deductibles, major medical is usually an insurance company's favorite kind of health policy. It can work well for you—as an insurance consumer—too. But you have to look at this coverage as one part of a larger approach to buying health insurance.

In other words, the major medical approach to hospitalization coverage is designed to provide you with protection against catastrophic expenses that are a genuine risk in today's world. You need to think of major medical as an approach because there are a lot of expenses that the plans don't cover. And you're going to have to fund those expenses somehow—either with out-of-pocket payments or some kind of supplemental insurance. We'll consider the options in this chapter.

The Concept

Major medical plans can be thought of as consisting of a bag of money, containing $1 million, $2 million, $5 million or an unlimited amount. The money is to be used to pay for covered medical expenses, either as an inpatient or as an outpatient. The only limitation is how much money is in the bag. Unlike a traditional indemnity policy with benefit amount limitations, major medical insurance is designed to provide a large sum of money from which to pay covered medical expenses.

Major medical plans are characterized by the following:

- deductibles
- co-insurance
- stop-loss provisions
- annual restoration provisions

We will consider each of these items in some detail.

Deductibles

The deductible associated with a major medical policy has essentially the same function as it does for any other type of insurance—whether health or car or homeowners. For example, you are responsible for the first $100 of medical expenses related to a hospital visit—your insurance company pays the excess covered medical expenses.

Most major medical plans will offer a variety of deductibles from $100 to $1,000—or even higher. Some high-risk policyholders—usually people with histories of health problems—pay as much as $5,000 or $10,000 deductibles. This is truly catastrophic coverage.

The deductible may be expressed as a calendar year deductible or as a per cause deductible. A calendar year deductible means that you satisfy the deductible once in a calendar year.

A per cause deductible is similar to the deductible found in the auto policy. Each time you ding a fender, you are responsible for a deductible. A per cause deductible basically states that each medical claim you incur will have a deductible requirement. Thus, if you had three claims, three deductibles would need to be satisfied before your insurance company would begin to pay benefits.

Example: If Scooter has three separate medical claims in a given year and his Allstate policy contains a $250 per cause deductible, then he must satisfy three separate deductibles before Allstate will pay his claim. If his policy with Allstate contains a calendar year deductible, he only has to pay one deductible to cover the entire year.

Another version of the calendar year deductible is the family deductible. Most plans will specify an individual deductible such as $250 and a family deductible equal to two or three times the individual deductible. So, if the plan had an individual deductible of $250 and a family deductible of $750, after the family incurred expenses totaling $750, there would be no further deductibles for the balance of that calendar year.

Most of the major medical plans contain a deductible carryover provision. If you haven't incurred any claims or received any benefits from the plan, expenses incurred in the last three months of a calendar year may be applied toward the new year's calendar deductible.

In this case, if Scooter has no claims in most of 1998 but does incur $100 of covered medical expenses in November 1998, he can apply that $100 toward the annual deductible for 1999.

Deductibles do have a large effect on the cost of major medical plans. A plan with a $100 deductible will cost considerably more than a plan with a $1,000 deductible. So, if you want to save premium dollars, select a plan with a higher deductible—it will reduce the cost of the premium.

Co-insurance Provisions

Once your deductible is satisfied, the major medical insurance company will then pay for covered medical expenses, on a co-insurance basis. (As we've seen, co-insurance—sometimes called co-payment—means that you and the insurance company split the cost of a claim. The company usually pays the larger part and you pay the smaller part.)

Co-insurance requirements are typically expressed as 80 percent to 20 percent, 70 percent to 30 percent, 60 percent to 40 percent, etc. So if you have a plan with an 80 percent to 20 percent co-insurance requirement, your insurance company will pay 80 percent of the covered expenses following the deductible and you are responsible for the additional 20 percent of the expenses.

Just as deductibles affect the cost of a plan, so too will co-insurance. An 80/20 percent co-insurance provision will carry a higher premium than a 70/30 percent or 60/40 percent co-insurance feature. If you need to keep your premium low, one way to meet this goal is to have a high deductible and a low co-insurance provision such as 60/40 percent.

This is another mechanism that insurance companies can use to limit the impact of insureds who have histories of health problems. If you've had heart bypass surgery and beaten a mild case of skin cancer, you may have to settle for a major medical policy that includes a high deductible—say, $5,000—and a heavy co-insurance split—say 60/40 percent.

Stop-loss Provision

The co-insurance requirement continues until you reach the policy's stop-loss point. The stop-loss is the point at which the insurance company begins to pay 100 percent of a claim. Without a stop-loss, you would be responsible for 20 percent of an indefinite amount such as $100,000 or even $1 million.

The stop-loss amount will vary. It could be reached at $2,500, $5,000 or $10,000 of covered expenses. For example, a plan with a $250 deductible and an 80/20 percent co-insurance split on the next $2,500 of covered expenses would result in a total out-of-pocket expense to the insured of $750—the $250 deductible plus 20 percent of $2,500. The stop-loss provision establishes the maximum out-of-pocket expense to you to be equal to the deductible plus the your co-insurance amount.

The out-of-pocket maximum is a major consideration when you are shopping for a policy. Regardless of the size of a potential claim, the most that you will have to pay out of your own pocket is the deductible and the co-insurance amount up to the stop-loss.

The stop-loss point is also a contributing factor in the policy's premium. The higher the stop-loss—the lower the premium. A stop-loss at $2,500 will cost more than a stop-loss at $10,000. Thus, if you want to keep the premium as low as possible, the formula becomes:

High deductible + low co-insurance + high stop-loss

Annual Restoration Provision

Let's look again at the major medical plan as consisting of a bag of money—holding a large amount, possibly $1 million, $2 million, etc. This sum is the maximum amount available for claims. You incur a claim subject to the plan's deductible and co-insurance requirements (including the stop-loss point). Whatever the total claim amount, it will be deducted from the bag of money leaving a smaller sum for future claims.

Example: Scooter has a $1 million dollar major medical plan with a $500 deductible, 80/20 percent co-insurance split up to $5,000, and 100 percent coverage thereafter. He's hit by a meteorite and incurs $300,000 in hospital costs recovering. After the deductible and co-insurance are paid, $294,100 is withdrawn from the bag of money—leaving $705,900 for future claims. If Scooter has no large claims for the rest of his life, he has nothing to worry about. But, if he's struck by lightning twelve months later, the money in the bag would dwindle to $411,800. If he breaks his back in a skiing accident a year after that, the money in the bag would be down to $117,700. And then he starts having trouble with his prostate....

The annual restoration provision puts back a certain amount of major medical dollars used each year. These amounts are generally small, such as $2,000, $3,000 or $5,000 per year.

If Scooter's plan contained a $5,000 restoration provision, one year after his claim (and, assuming he doesn't have such a hard-luck existence) the total amount available for future claims would be increased to $710,900. After two years it would be $715,900—and so forth.

The size of a claim is usually several times larger than the amount restored. Many view this as a token reassurance that some sum of money will be in the plan for claims. If the plan only has a $1 million lifetime maximum, it is possible to exhaust this sum with a major illness such as a prolonged battle with cancer. To offset this disadvantage, many insurers today provide major medical plans with $2 million lifetime maximums or unlimited maximums.

A $2 million dollar maximum is more realistic with regard to the size of typical claims. Even with a major prolonged illness, it would be difficult to exhaust benefits of $2 million.

The following chart defines the major medical concepts we've considered so far.

Chapter 4

MAJOR MEDICAL INSURANCE

Deductible	Co-insurance	Stop Loss
Must be satisfied before any benefits are paid	The insured pays a small part of the claims	The insurer pays 100% when stop loss is reached

Usual, Customary, and Reasonable Charges

Co-insurance amounts are based on what the insurance company considers the usual, customary, and reasonable (UCR) expenses or charges. In addition, when the stop-loss is reached, the insurer will pay 100 percent of the UCR expenses. The introduction of reasonable and customary language into the policy means you may incur some additional out-of-pocket expenses—if the expenses incurred are not considered reasonable and customary.

The UCR amounts are determined by the insurance company. Periodically, the services provided and charges made by doctors and hospitals are reviewed by the insurance company. The review takes into account geographical differences that allow for differences in the charges relative to the provider's overhead expenses, location, etc. The insurance company then establishes UCR charges for specific services in a specific geographical area.

Example: Julie has an tonsillectomy performed in a small farm community in central Nebraska. She is charged $1,500 for the procedure. By coincidence, Julie's friend Suzy has the same procedure performed at a New York City hospital and her charge is $2,000. It's possible that Julie's incurred expense of $1,500 for the tonsillectomy would be considered reasonable and customary by her insurance company. It is also conceivable that Suzy's $2,000 charge would be reasonable and customary for the New York City area. If so, their claims would be paid in full by their respective insurance companies.

On the other hand, assume that Julie incurs a $2,000 charge for her tonsillectomy. She hasn't reached the stop-loss point but has satisfied her deductible. Julie's insurance company will pay 80 percent of $1,500—the UCR charge—or $1,200. Julie is responsible for 20 percent ($300) and now she must contend with a $500 excess charge. Her insurance company views the $500 as excess or unreasonable for that part of Nebraska. Julie has to pay $800 out of her own pocket to cover the expense. The excess is an additional out-of-pocket expense for Julie which is not counted by the insurer towards the stop-loss point or any other provision of the policy.

What can someone dealing with a UCR dispute do? One option—the one that insurance companies and health care providers hope you will choose—is simply to pay the difference and forget it. Another option is to appeal the decision with the insurance company's internal review structure. A third is to file a complaint with state regulatory authorities, though major medical insurance companies are usually allowed wide discretion in setting UCR fee schedules.

But there's a less contentious approach that often works. Explain to your health care provider that your insurance company uses a UCR limit that's lower than the fee you've been charged. If you back this argument up with the insurance company's paperwork, you may be able convince the provider to bring the bill in line with the UCR fee schedule.

Often, doctors and hospitals would rather coordinate their fees with an insurance company's UCR schedule than fight it. They don't want to be identified with difficult claims. This sometimes brings scrutiny and slower payments.

In Julie's case, she could tell her doctor that her insurance company considers $1,500 to be a UCR fee for her tonsillectomy and will only reimburse that amount. The doctor may agree to accept the insurance company's reimbursement and Julie will only owe the $300 co-insurance portion. If the doctor insists that the full amount be paid, Julie could simply ignore the bill—and the doctor's collection efforts which will likely follow. There is always a chance that the doctor will give up. But that's a risky approach that most people should probably avoid to protect their credit ratings.

The problem with UCR disputes is that a doctor may not consider a high fee to be unreasonable—only the insurance company does. And you are caught in the middle. Unfortunately, there is no simple answer when the insurance company deems a charge to be unreasonable.

One obvious preventive measure is to find out the cost of a procedure before it becomes a claim and then check with the insurance company to determine how much of this charge will be paid. This gives you the chance to discuss the fee with your doctor before incurring any expense. And your doctor will probably be more inclined to reduce the fee before it becomes a claims matter.

Another alternative is to find a doctor or surgeon who will perform the surgery for the UCR charge as determined by the insurance company. However, this is probably an unacceptable option because, if you are considering having surgery or some similar medical work, you have enough to worry about without shopping for a bargain from an unknown doctor. People usually take the position that they buy major medical insurance because they'd prefer to have surgery done by their own doctors.

Therefore—as difficult as it may be—the best strategy is to get a copy of your insurance company's UCR fee schedule to your provider before you undergo major treatment.

Major Medical vs. Basic Medical

For many, major medical is the most feasible health care plan in spite of its deductible and co-insurance provisions. The "bag of money" concept works better—is more affordable or available—in the present health care environment than a pure indemnity plan's first-dollar coverage approach.

An important point: With the major medical approach, not only inpatient expenses are covered but outpatient expenses are, too. Outpatient diagnostic services, doctors office calls, etc., are covered expenses under the major medical plan. The same bag of money used to pay inpatient expenses can be used to cover outpatient expenses subject to the plan's deductible and co-insurance features. In addition, the major medical approach may not involve the limitations of time and money that a basic plan does.

The major medical plan will have a lifetime maximum benefit such as $1 million or $2 million. Some plans are even written with an unlimited lifetime maximum. This form of limitation is much more workable than one which limits dollars for specific expenses such as surgery and room and board expenses. It is unlikely that an insured will "run out of money" with the major medical plan.

With regard to the cost of the plans, the premium for a major medical plan could be less than the premium for a basic medical expense plan. This is especially true if the individual is relatively young and has no dependents. The size of the deductible and the co-insurance provisions can usually result in a lower premium than for a plan which has no deductibles or co-insurance.

Comprehensive Medical Expense Policies

As we've already seen, major medical coverage is considered hospitalization insurance. It doesn't cover all medical expenses—the way that traditional indemnity coverage does. What do you do about these other expenses? Paying for them out-of-pocket is the simplest option. But you need to be cash-rich to do this. So, most people will look for some kind of insurance to add on to their major medical.

An additional challenge to a smart insurance consumer is that many companies don't sell traditional indemnity health coverage that starts with the first dollar. These companies force policyholders to start with major medical and build additional coverage from there.

So, in some situations, you may be faced with the prospect of buying a comprehensive medical expense plan. This kind of insurance adds coverage for basic—and not necessarily hospital-related—medical expenses to the major medical coverage. As we saw in the previous chapter, basic medical expenses are sometimes insured on a stand-alone basis.

The comprehensive plan is simply a combination of:

Basic Medical Expen.se + Major Medical

This may seem like a long way to walk around the insurance block in order to get back to something like the traditional indemnity coverage we've considered earlier. It is. The long walk is a testament to how convoluted insurance coverage can be.

The comprehensive plan consists of a block of first dollar benefits followed by a deductible and a typical major medical plan. This plan might specify that 100 percent of the first $5,000 or $10,000 of reasonable and customary expenses will be covered. Once this bundle of first dollar benefits is exhausted, you must satisfy a deductible, usually referred to as a corridor deductible, and then the major medical benefits are activated.

All of the provisions common to a basic hospitalization plan as well as the provisions and concepts related to major medical plans, ie., deductibles, co-insurance, stop loss, etc., are found in this type of plan.

The following table illustrates key features of a comprehensive medical expense plan.

Comprehensive Medical Expense Plan

Basic Medical Plan

100% of the first $10,000 of expenses

80/20% co-insurance on the first $5,000

Corridor Deductible

$500

Major Medical Plan

No deductible or co-insurance

100% thereafter to the policy maximum

The question raised by the comprehensive plan is whether or not you would be better off with this plan or simply a "straight" major medical plan. Does the block of first dollar benefits really enhance your overall protection?

To answer these questions, let's use the same $20,000 hospital bill just used to reflect the payment of major medical expenses. We'll use the comprehensive plan illustrated above.

Calculation of the comprehensive benefits would be as follows:

Total Expense:	$20,000
100% of the first $10,000:	$10,000
Balance of $10,000: ($10,000 - $500 deductible)	$9,500
80% of $5,000:	$4,000
100% of balance ($4,500):	$4,500

Total benefits provided by the comprehensive plan are $18,500 which is the same 92 percent of covered expenses we saw with the regular major medical plan. In other words, as long as the expenses exceed the package of first dollar benefits ($10,000) and the deductible and co-insurance amounts (an additional $5,500), there is no difference in the benefits provided.

There usually will be a difference in the premium, since a higher premium will be charged for the block of first dollar benefits in the plan. You are getting into your insurance company's pockets immediately (up to $10,000) when a claim is incurred, so you will have to pay for this by means of a higher premium.

A regular major medical plan will do essentially the same job as the higher-priced comprehensive plan, unless the claim is relatively small ($10,000 or less). The first dollar benefits will cover the relatively small claim without any deductible or co-insurance.

In small claim situations, the extra premium for the comprehensive plan has to be weighed against the likelihood of a small claim of a few thousand dollars. By today's health care costs, it is difficult to spend a few days in a hospital, have surgery and not incur expenses exceeding $10,000.

Comprehensive plans vary, but generally cover the same kinds of services. Some of these include:

- professional services of doctors of medicine and osteopathy and other recognized medical practitioners
- hospital charges for semiprivate room and board and other necessary services and supplies
- surgical charges
- services of registered nurses and, in some cases, licensed practical nurses
- home health care
- physical therapy
- anesthetics and their administration
- x-rays and other diagnostic laboratory procedures
- x-ray or radium treatment
- oxygen and other gases and their administration
- blood transfusions, including the cost of blood when charged
- medicine requiring a prescription
- specified ambulance services
- rental of durable mechanical equipment required for therapeutic use

- artificial limbs and other prosthetic appliances, except replacement of such appliances
- casts, splints, braces and crutches
- rental of a wheelchair or hospital bed

Summary

Major medical coverage is considered by many people with histories of health problems to be a realistic and comprehensive approach to getting indemnity-type coverage for health care expenses. The major medical plan provides a supply of money to be used over the lifetime of the insured. After the deductible is satisfied, you and your insurance company co-insure claims expenses by means of the plan's co-insurance requirements.

Co-insurance only applies to a specific amount of expenses up to the stop-loss amount. Once this figure is reached, your losses stop and your insurance company pays the claim in full thereafter.

> Major medical plans are characterized by deductibles, co-insurance and stop-loss provisions.

Major medical plans usually contain an annual restoration provision whereby a small amount of money is restored to the plan each year after plan dollars have been used to pay medical expenses.

Expenses are covered based on the premise of UCR fees. The plan's co-insurance provisions will provide coverage for those expenses deemed reasonable and customary by geographical reason per the research of the insurance company.

Some people supplement major medical coverage with basic medical expense coverage to create a comprehensive health insurance package. This somewhat complex approach is made necessary by the fact that many people can't qualify for or afford traditional indemnity coverage—and the fact that some insurance companies don't sell traditional indemnity coverage.

Managed Care

Managed Care

The broad health coverage provided by traditional insurance plans provides little incentive for efficient cost-effective health care delivery. Starting in the 1980s, it became clear that too much money was being spent on health care in the United States. One response from insurers and providers was to reorganize the health care delivery system into a form of managed care.

Managed care imposes controls on the use of health care services, the providers of health care services, usually through health maintenance organizations (HMOs) or preferred provider organizations (PPOs).

Managed care plans can be organized as for-profit (commercial) corporations or non-profit corporations. In most scenarios, however, a managed care plan is a for-profit corporation with responsibilities to stockholders that take precedence over responsibilities to you. The HMO directly and indirectly controls the amount of health care that the doctors in its network are allowed to provide to you.

What's worse is that, if you switch your insurance to a managed care plan and your personal physician isn't in the network, you probably can't continue to go to the same doctor. And, even if he or she is a member, your office visits still may be restricted—particularly if your doctor is a specialist.

Most managed care plans require you to choose a primary care doctor from their list of doctors. The primary care doctor, also called a gatekeeper, controls your access to medical care. And unless your primary care doctor decides your medical problem is outside his or her own realm of expertise, you will not be able to see a specialist.

The roots of managed care go back to prepaid health plans of the 19th century, but many of the concepts used in today's health care system were embraced in ancient times. King Hammurabi of Babylon incorporated these same managed care concepts in the Codex Hammurabi—a huge stone stele—around 1700 B.C. Managed Care pointed to several similarities between the Codex and what we know today as managed care, including:

- rates set for various procedures: general surgery, eye surgery, setting fractures, curing diseased muscles and other specific health care services
- fees set according to a sliding scale based on ability to pay
- property owners to pay for health care for their households
- objective outcome measurement standards to assure quality of care
- outcomes information management to include data collection and evaluation
- patient's rights to be publicized, explained and made known to all

The *Codex Hammurabi* indicates that during this time Babylonians could expect treatment not unlike that envisioned by the various versions of the current patient's Bill of Rights.

How an HMO Works

Today's health maintenance organizations are a relatively recent service approach to providing prepaid doctor and hospital care. Their growth has been encouraged by rising health care costs and federal legislation.

An HMO is an entity that contracts with medical facilities, physicians, employers and sometimes individual patients to provide medical care to a group of individuals. This care is usually paid for by a company or other group at a fixed price per patient. Patients generally do not have any significant "out-of-pocket" expenses.

The principal objectives of HMOs are similar to the managed care health system of the Codex of Hammurabi, in that they aim to reduce medical expenses by:

- stressing preventive medicine—physical exams and diagnostic procedures
- reducing the number of unnecessary hospital admissions
- reducing the average number of days per hospital visit
- reducing duplication of benefits
- saving on administrative costs

Federal employee benefit law passed during the 1970s requires employers who offer health care benefits to offer enrollment in an HMO as an alternative to an indemnity plan. Employers falling under this Act are those that:

- have 25 or more employees and are within the service area of a federally qualified HMO
- are paying at least minimum wage
- offer a health plan to their employees

HMOs are sometimes owned and controlled by commercial insurance companies. However, many are independently owned. Blue Cross and Blue Shield plans—or their affiliates—own and operate several dozen of the largest HMOs in the U.S. Other organizers of HMOs include governments, hospitals, employers, unions, consumer groups and local communities.

HMOs must operate within a specified geographical area known as the service area. The service area must be approved by the state Department of Insurance and all members of the HMO must reside in the prescribed service area. The service area is usually a city, or a part of a city and occasionally an entire state. In the later 1990s, service areas began to play a diminished role.

HMOs must be state qualified (able to provide services within a single state or states) or federally qualified (able to provide services in specified areas throughout the nation for national contracts like the United Auto Workers, Teamsters or government employees). If an HMO is federally qualified, it must also be state qualified in the states where it serves members obtained through a national contract.

HMOs provide service through one or more of three "models" of operation:

The Group Practice Model (GPM), also known as the Medical Group Model, is composed of a group of physicians of varying specializations practicing in one facility. It is similar to a clinic-type operation. Under the group practice model, your HMO contracts with a medical group to provide you with health care services.

If the medical group provides services to HMO members only it is called a closed panel medical group. Under a closed panel HMO, physicians are usually salaried employees of the HMO and work at a clinic owned by the HMO. If the medical group provides services to HMO members in addition to other, nonmember patients, it is called an open panel medical group. Under an open panel, doctors are not salaried and treat HMO subscribers in their own offices. Generally, you would not need to go farther than the medical group for the health care, unless of course hospitalization is needed.

The medical group refers you internally, within the medical group, to physicians of differing specializations as needed (i.e. pediatrician, surgeon etc.). Special arrangements can be made if a specialist of a particular type of medicine is needed and not a part of the medical group. Your HMO also contracts with hospitals in the area to provide you with services that are not available through the medical group, or if you require surgery, etc.

The Staff Model health care delivery system is actually owned, operated, staffed etc., by your HMO. The HMO controls the physician group, and the physicians and other health care professionals are employees of the HMO. The HMO could also build a medical group facility and hire physicians to staff it and provide health care services to members.

The key element of a Staff Model is that the HMO's own employees and facilities are being used to provide health care services to the HMO's members.

An **Independent Practice Association Model (IPA)** is a network of individually practicing physicians who contract with your HMO to provide you with health care services. Unlike the Group Practice Model, an IPA's physicians are located throughout a geographic area and are operated independently of each other.

If you select an IPA, you would receive a list of physicians of varying specializations to choose from. Initially, you would choose your own primary care physician (usually a general practitioner, or if for a child oftentimes a pediatrician) and visit this physician for treatment.

However, if your primary care physician cannot render treatment, then he or she will refer you to the appropriate specialist within the IPA network. Like the Group Practice Model, the physicians of an IPA may utilize hospitals affiliated (that is, contracted) with your HMO to render services not available at their independent practices.

Physicians who are part of an IPA treat patients on an open panel (HMO members and nonmembers) or closed panel (HMO members only) basis, depending on their contract with the HMO.

Co-payments

Many HMOs and other managed care plans require members to make a co-payment when they get treatment. A co-payment is a specific dollar amount, or percentage of the cost of a service that you must pay in order to receive a basic health care service.

> Co-payments are due every time you visit a health care provider.

Example: you may be required to pay a $10 co-payment for an office visit to your physician, or you might be required to pay a 30 percent co-payment (30 percent of the cost of the services) for alcohol and drug rehabilitation.

Some HMOs don't require any co-payment for a considerable number of their services. Co-payments for alcohol and drug rehabilitation, and services for mental and emotional disorders are usually expressed as a percentage of the cost of the service and are, therefore, more costly to the member. Co-payments for supplemental services are often considerably more than for basic services.

HMO Exclusions and Limitations

Exclusions or limitaions are used to either limit a benefit provided or specifically exclude a type of coverage, benefit, medical procedure, etc. HMOs may not exclude and limit benefits as readily as commercial insurance companies. This is usually because the rationale of an HMO is to provide comprehensive health care coverage.

Benefits that your HMO may exclude from coverage include: eye examinations and refractions for persons over age 17, eyeglasses or contact lenses resulting from an eye examination, dental services, prescription drugs (other than those administered in a hospital), long-term physical therapy (over 90 days) and out-of-area benefits (other than emergency services).

Your HMO is required to have a complaint system, often called a grievance procedure, to resolve any written complaints that you may have. They provide forms for written complaints, including the address and telephone number of where complaints should be directed. Additionally, your HMO must notify you of any time limits applying to a complaint.

Complaints must be resolved within 180 days of being filed with the HMO (with a few exceptions). They may be resolved through binding arbitration if so specified by the HMO.

Enrollment

Your HMO must provide you with evidence of coverage within 60 days of enrollment. The evidence of coverage should include your coverages and benefits (including your required co-payments), benefit limits, exclusions, and specified conversion privileges. It should also include:

> Evidence of coverage is equivalent to a Certificate of Insurance for standard insurance policies.

- the name, address, and telephone number of the HMO
- the effective date and term of coverage
- a list of providers and a description of the service area
- terms and conditions for termination
- a complaint system
- a 31-day grace period for premium payment provision
- a coordination of benefits provision
- incontestability clause
- a provision on eligibility requirements for membership in the HMO

Other provisions may also be found in the evidence of coverage, but those outlined above must be included.

HMO Benefits

HMO benefits are not limited to treatment resulting from illness or injury, but include preventative measures like routine physical examinations and programs for quitting smoking, losing weight and managing blood pressure.

HMOs provide a wide range of health care services. These required services are referred to as basic health care services. And any services or benefits provided by your HMO in excess of the basic services are referred to as supplemental health care services. Your HMO must provide you with a list of the basic services that are covered under the plan. The following is an example:

> HMO members pay a set fee, usually on a monthly basis, which entitles them to a broad definition of "necessary health care."

- inpatient hospital and physician services for at least 90 days per calendar year for treatment of injury and illness or injury

If inpatient treatment is for mental, emotional or nervous disorders—including alcohol and drug rehabilitation treatment—services may be limited to 30 days per calendar year. Treatment for alcohol and drug rehabilitation and treatment may be restricted to a 90-day lifetime limit.

- outpatient medical services when prescribed by a physician and rendered in a non-hospital health care facility (i.e. physician's office, member's home, etc.) including diagnostic services, treatment services, short-term physical therapy and rehabilitation services, laboratory and x-ray services and outpatient surgery
- preventative health services, including well child care from birth, eye and ear examinations for children

under age 18 and periodic health evaluations and immunizations

- in- and out-of-area emergency services, including medically necessary ambulance services, available on an inpatient or an outpatient basis 24 hours per day, seven days per week

Supplemental health care services may take the form of additional coverages over and above those provided as basic, or additional amounts of the basic benefits already provided.

Guidelines Plans Must Follow

HMOs, like traditional indemnity insurance companies, cannot engage in certain types of business practices, policies, etc. Specifically, your HMO is prohibited from excluding your pre-existing conditions from coverage, from unfairly discriminating against you based on age, sex, health status, race, color, creed, national origin or marital status.

Your HMO is also prohibited from terminating your coverage for reasons other than:

- nonpayment of premiums or co-payments
- fraud or deception
- a violation of contract terms
- failure to meet or continue to meet eligibility requirements
- a termination of the group contract under which you are covered

Because an HMO provides service benefits rather than reimbursement benefits, they are required to follow guidelines prescribed by the Insurance Department to assure quality service to members.

These guidelines specify the requirements for reasonable hours of operation and after-hours emergency health care and standards to insure that sufficient personnel will be available to attend to your needs. The guidelines also require adequate arrangements to provide inpatient hospital services for basic health care and a requirement that the services of specialists be provided as a basic health care service.

Problems Plans Face

Consumer advocates made much during the late 1980s and early 1990s about the harsh treatment HMOs give members. They told stories—many factual, some exaggerated—about so-called "drive through deliveries" (women sent home hours after giving birth), assembly-line surgeries and miserly gatekeepers. One of the legitimate issues raised by this muck-racking: Some plans put business-oriented administrators—rather than doctors—in decision-making positions with regard to the delivery of care.

An impersonal approach has been the source of many problems for HMOs in the public mind. So, most of the plans have begun using networks of so-called "individual practitioners." In these individual practice associations (IPAs), you will get your care in a specific physician's office. More than half the people enrolled in HMOs are in IPAs.

At first glance, managed care appears better than a traditional indemnity plan, on average, at getting doctors to follow basic practices that safeguard health. But critics say that oftentimes, the companies don't follow through to make sure the doctors are tackling problems aggressively.

More often than not, managed care has been criticized for compromising the quality of care just to cut costs. One common, highly controversial techniques that managed care has been criticized for is the use of bonuses or incentive pools to reward doctors for not wasting medical resources. And unfortunately, these incentive pools sometimes cause doctors to deny appropriate care.

Some industry experts suggest that what's most unnerving about managed care is that the care isn't necessarily worse than before, but it brings into focus what a highly variable, random approach doctors and managed care companies take toward medicine. In fact, some researchers suggest that there is some evidence that managed care has nudged doctors toward producing the most cost-effective outcomes.

Recently, the federal government has begun to draft laws which will limit the limits—reducing the discretion HMOs can use in delivering expensive health care services. These proposals answer the outrages raised by consumer advocates, but they may end up destroying the beneficial cost controls that the plans have mastered.

Preferred Provider Organizations (PPOs)

Unlike HMOs, PPOs do not utilize primary care gatekeepers. A single physician does not manage an individual's health care services. PPOs—a cross between regular fee-for-service plans and HMOs—are designed to provide you with increased benefits if you use doctors and hospitals within its network.

Commercial insurers implemented PPOs as an answer to some of the negative aspects of HMOs, such as a the limited choice of physicians. A PPO is a nice compromise if you don't want to pay for traditionally expensive fee-for-service coverage, but want more choice than an HMO offers. And a growing number of people are making that choice, according to a survey by benefits consulting firm Foster Higgins.

According to Foster Higgins, employers are continuing to enroll a growing number of workers in managed care plans— however, only in those plans that retain an employee's choice of physician. More than half (53 percent) of the nation's employees were enrolled in a managed care plan in 1993, up from 48 percent in 1992, and PPOs captured the largest share of the managed care market, with 27 percent of employees enrolled in 1993.

Small and large employers continue to add PPOs. The number of smaller employers offering PPOs increased from

21 percent in 1992 to 24 percent in 1993. Among large employers, PPOs grew form 33 percent to 36 percent.

Here's how a PPO works. Your insurance company, as they do in HMOs, contracts with certain physicians and provides a "preferred provider" network of doctors and specialists that you can choose to go to. However, unlike HMOs, you don't have to go to the doctors in the preferred provider network, and you don't have to get referrals from your primary care physician to see a specialist.

However, if you are in a PPO, you will be encouraged to use the preferred provider to keep costs down for both you and your insurance company. If you do, you will pay for services with co-payments, just like an HMO, or you receive a higher co-insurance amount than you would if you used a doctor that is not in the preferred provider organization.

Example: If Joan used a doctor in the PPO Network, she might get 90 percent co-insurance, so she would only have to pay 10 percent of the cost of the medical service, and she would have a low deductible (the part that she 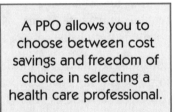 must pay first before the insurance company starts paying anything).

A PPO allows you to choose between cost savings and freedom of choice in selecting a health care professional.

Generally, a deductible for PPO coverage ranges between $150 and $300 per year. If you don't use the PPO network often, you might only have 70 percent co-insurance and a higher deductible. That would mean that you'd pay a higher deductible (somewhere between $300 and $500 per year per individual) and 30 percent of costs after that.

PPOs are considered to be closer to indemnity plans than managed care, since the insurance company pays discounted rates for medical services without becoming overly involved in health care decisions about the treatments rendered.

Why Some People Like PPOs Better Than HMOs

PPOs are a better choice than fee-for-service plans if you don't make a lot of money but you want to have some flexibility in your choice of a physician. They are also good if you have built a relationship with a physician not in the network and want to continue that relationship. You can still use preferred providers for other services and keep seeing your specialist.

PPOs are also good when you know you will exceed the deductible amount. However, if you don't exceed the deductible, you will basically be getting no value out of your insurance because the deductible amount must come out of your pocket before your insurance company starts paying.

Exclusive Provider Organizations (EPOs)

Exclusive provider organizations are a type of PPO in which you can use a particular provider, instead of choosing from a list of preferred providers. In this situation, providers are not paid a salary but are paid on a fee-for-service basis.

EPOs are characterized by a primary physician who monitors care and makes referrals to a network of providers (this is the same gatekeeper concept), strong utilization management, experience rating and simplified claims processing. EPOs can serve as an alternative to or companion to HMOs and PPOs.

Open Ended Plans

Another managed care alternative to an HMO, an open ended HMO (also known as a "leaky HMO" and "point-of-service HMO"), is a hybrid arrangement whereby you can use non-HMO providers at any time and receive indemnity benefits which are subject to higher deductible and co-insurance amounts.

The out-of-pocket cost to you (and probably your employer, too) is higher, but the arrangement allows you to remain in control in choosing a health care provider.

Multiple Option Plans

You might want to look into a multiple option plan. This type of plan is an integrated health plan that includes services of an HMO, PPO, EPO and a traditional indemnity plan—all of which are administered by a single vendor (usually a traditional insurance company).

And there are many variations of managed care systems, including: point of service plans (POSs), physician hospital organizations (PHOs), practice management organizations (PMOs), and provider-owned networks. Most of these alternatives combine the mechanical controls of HMOs, the flexibility of PPOs and some kind of provider (that is, physician) ownership. The goal of these alternative managed care plans is to reap the benefits of cost control while keeping doctors in on the decision-making process.

Indemnity Insurance vs. Managed Care

There is a high level of concern over the practices of managed care providers. Managed care is known for its atrocities: gatekeepers refusing to give referrals, HMO requirements to notify or get permission from a primary care physician, financial incentives for physicians who restrict care for cost containment purposes, "gag" clauses prohibiting doctors from discussing expensive treatments, drive-through deliveries, drive-through mastectomies, and capitated payment systems.

In fact, a report sponsored by the Patient Access to Specialty Care Coalition—a group comprised of national organizations representing consumers and providers of medical services—went so far as to say that most patients trust the federal government and auto mechanics more than managed care companies.

The number of large employers offering a POS plan also grew in 1993. Some 15 percent of large employers offered a POS plan in 1993, up from 10 percent in 1992. And, enrollment in POS plans grew to 9 percent of employees in 1993, up from 6 percent the previous year. However, POS plans are rare among smaller employers, offered by only 4 percent the report said.

While there was some increase in the number of employers offering HMOs to employees in 1993, enrollment remained unchanged. Among larger employers, 46 percent offered an HMO in 1993, compared to 43 percent in 1992. Some 21 percent of smaller employers offered an HMO in 1993, which was unchanged from 1992. HMO enrollment also remained stable between 1992 and 1993 at 19 percent of employees.

Beginning in the 1990s, various political groups in Washington, D.C. started lobbying for various versions of a so-called Patients' Bill of Rights to be passed into law. While the different plans included specific details of their own, they tended to share some basic points.

The proposals tended to eliminate many of the cost-control mechanisms that managed care plans use to keep their coverage less expensive than traditional indemnity insurance. Among the common targets: gatekeeper referral systems, appeals boards made up of administrators (rather than doctors) and restrictive lists of approved providers. (For more details on this issue, see Chapter 13.)

Summary

In the early 1990s, managed care plans surpassed indemnity plans as the most common mechanism for delivering health care services in the United States. Although the plans may seem like the innovation, they are in fact the rule.

Some facts about managed care in the United States, as of 1998:

- Number of HMOs in the United States: 574
- Number of PPOs in the United States: 1,036
- Number of Americans in HMOs: 51.0 million
- Number of Americans in PPOs: 50.2 million
- Percentage of insured employees (working in firms with at least 10 employees) in managed care health plans: 66
- Percentage of doctors with at least one managed care contract: 75
- Percentage of doctors with at least one HMO contract: 48
- Percentage of HMOs that are for-profit: 69
- Percentage of HMOs that are not-for-profit: 31
- Percentage of HMO members in for-profit plans: 58
- Percentage of HMO members in not-for-profit plans: 42
- Percentage of HMOs that offer nutrition courses: 87
- Percentage of HMOs that offer smoking cessation courses: 67

Ultimately, the biggest issue facing managed care in the United States is whether all the talk of a Patient's Bill of Rights will lead federal regulators or the court system (federal or state) to erode HMOs and PPOs so much that they cease to have any cost-saving advantage over other health coverage plans.

An example of this erosion came up in early 1999, when a California jury ordered Aetna/U.S. Health Care to pay $116 million in punitive damages for refusing to cover experimental treatment for a cancer patient—who eventually died.

In 1992, David Goodrich was diagnosed with a rare form of stomach cancer. Doctors in the Aetna HMO recommended that Goodrich undergo high-dose chemotherapy and a bone-marrow transplant. But the system's administrators denied the coverage.

However, nothing in the plan's handbook—the main document about coverage issues that members receieved—said that the treatments recommended by its own doctors were excluded.

One California-based managed care expert summed up the issues wrapped in the big verdict: "This shows the issue that is driving the consumer debate is the fear that plans are looking over the shoulders of doctors and are denying what a doctor perceives to be medically necessary."

Managed care advocates would argue that the problems reflected in the Aetna/U.S.Health Care case had been resolved years before. But the tide of public opinion was continuing to flow against managed care cost controls.

Group
Health Plan
Coverage

6

Group Health Plan Coverage

Health coverage is packaged for sale to both individuals and groups. Most people in the United States get their coverage in a group package. And most of the group plans are sold to companies and their employees.

Business health care spending increased more than six-fold between 1965 and 1994. With medical costs on the rise through the 1980s and 1990s, various management surveys show that healthcare expenditures remain the single most important concern for U.S. employers.

Although group and individual health insurance policies share many of the same policy provisions, there are significant differences. In an individual policy, the contract is between you and your insurance company. In a group policy, the contract is between the company and your employer, union, trust or other sponsoring organization.

A caveat: Your family members may be covered under both group and individual policies. But you should determine how they will be covered before signing on to either kind of policy.

While group policies may have fewer limitations, they do have one important drawback. If you change jobs, you may no longer be covered under your last employer's group policy. However, individual health insurance contracts continue regardless of change of employment.

The Group Insurance Contract

A group insurance policy, or master policy is issued to the policyowner—usually your employer, association, union, or trust, etc. And if you are covered under the group policy you are issued a certificate of insurance. The certificate lists what the policy covers, and explains such things as how to file a claim, the term of insurance, and the right to convert from group coverage to an individual policy.

Many of the group health insurance contracts features are similar to the contract features of group life insurance.

Group health insurance is generally subject to experience rating, under which the premium modification factor is determined by the experience of the group as a whole. In contrast, individual policies may be subject to community rating, under which the insurance company's overall experience is adjusted in different areas to reflect variations in local costs for doctor and hospital services.

Employee Group

An employee group policy may be issued to an employer (or to the trustee of a fund established by an employer) where insurance is secured for the benefit of the employees, or for persons other than the employer.

> The employer is the policyowner, and establishes the eligible class of employees to be covered under the group policy.

Usually, this classification will include all full-time employees (including the employer). Further, the classification can also specify full-time, salaried, non-union employees. By classifying the employee group in this manner, the employer is legally able to exclude certain groups of employees (part-time, union, etc.) from the eligible class of covered employees. The eligible class of employees may also include retired employees.

Union or Association Group

An association, including a labor union, must have the following characteristics to be considered an authorized group:

- have a constitution and bylaws
- be organized and maintained for purposes other than obtaining insurance
- have insurance for the purpose of covering members or employees for the benefit of persons other than the association or its officers or trustees (in this context, the term "employee" may include retired employees)

Trustee Group

A policy may be issued to the trustees of a "trust group" if the fund has been:

- established by two or more employers in the same or related field
- established by one or more labor unions or associations (this is also known as a "Taft-Hartley Trust")

> Group health coverages track closely with benefits available under individual coverages.

The trustees are the policyholder of the plan which covers the eligible employees. Such plan must not be for the benefit of the employer, union or association. The individuals who may be considered "employees" as defined by this section are the same as those previously listed under Employee Group.

Disability Income

Group disability income coverage provides for loss of income benefits due to a disability caused by an accident or sickness. The amount of benefits paid is usually a percentage of your weekly or monthly compensation, such as 60 percent or 70 percent. This is intended to encourage you—the disabled employee—to recover and return to work. If 100 percent of compensation were provided, there would be no such incentive for you to return to work.

Benefits are payable following the policy's elimination period (EP). The EP is a waiting period during which you must be totally disabled as defined by the policy. An EP can be 7, 15, 30 days or longer.

Group benefits may be short-term or long-term. Short-term benefits are usually payable for up to one or two years—though usually one year. Short-term policies usually have short elimination periods such as 15 or 30 days.

Long-term disability (LTD) benefits are usually paid out for longer benefit periods such as five years or until you turn 65. Generally, LTD policies will have longer elimination periods, such as 90 or 180 days.

Accidental Death and Dismemberment

Accidental death and dismemberment coverage pays specified amounts for specific injuries or for death. Benefits are only payable if the injury or death is caused by accident. Injuries must result in specific losses such as loss of sight, arms, legs or feet. This coverage can be written as a separate policy or as part of a policy providing other group health insurance benefits.

Medical Expense

Basic group medical expense policies usually provide benefits for inpatient services such as hospital room and board costs, surgical expenses and miscellaneous charges.

Outpatient (out of the hospital) expenses are usually not covered.

Basic group plans have limitations. Usually, benefits are limited to a specified amount. Room and board charges may be limited to $300 or $400 per day for example. Surgical benefits are usually factors of a surgical schedule which specifies the maximum surgical benefit to be paid. Miscellaneous benefits (private duty nurses, bandages, medication, in-hospital x-rays, lab work, etc.) are usually limited by an amount equal to 10 or 20 times the daily room and board rate.

Basic plans are also limited in terms of time. Most plans will specify that policy benefits will be paid for 30 days or possibly up to 365 days.

Because of these limitations, basic medical expense plans usually do not cover your medical expenses in full. As a result, you will be responsible for certain out-of-pocket expenses.

In contrast to basic group medical plans, group major medical policies provide more comprehensive benefits. Group major medical will "limit" benefits normally to what is reasonable and customary as opposed to a specific dollar amount. In essence, you are provided with a sum of money to cover medical expenses. Most insurers require 75 percent or more of the eligible members to participate. Under a non-contributory plan, the employer pays the entire premium. The insurance companies in this case require 100 percent participation.

The minimum participation requirement is to help guard against adverse selection. If a free choice were given, many people in good health might not choose the insurance, whereas many in poor health most certainly would.

Group medical coverage may cost less than individual policies depending on the ages and dependent status of the participants. If you are single, you can usually purchase individual coverage for a smaller premium than if comparable coverage was obtained under a group policy.

When a group policy is rated, the premium may be higher or lower than individual coverage because everyone in the group is paying for every other group member. If the ages of the participants are relatively high, the premiums will be high. A single person, age 21, will consequently pay a relatively higher premium (due to the age of the group) than he or she might pay on an individual policy basis. An individual policy is rated on the age and insurability of the applicant, not an entire group.

On the other hand, a married person with several children would probably find that the group premium would be less than an individual family premium. On an individual basis, this person must "pay by the head"—must pay a premium for each covered family member. Usually, a group policy will charge a family rate regardless of the number of dependents the participant may have. This is a good deal for people with families.

Credit Health Coverage

Not all forms of group health insurance are cost effective. Credit health insurance is usually written as a group disability income contract although it could also be an individual policy. The purpose of credit health is to provide payment of your debt if you are disabled due to accident or sickness.

The creditor is the policyowner—or your employer—and you are the debtor. Disability benefits equal to your debt are paid directly to the creditor in the event that you become disabled in accordance with policy provisions. These benefits are usually paid on a monthly basis as long as the debt remains, and you are sick. By most reckoning, credit health coverage—even purchased on a group basis—is not a very cost-effective kind of insurance.

Self-insured Plans

If claim costs are fairly consistent, your employer may consider a self-funded health care plan. With a self-funded plan your employer, not an insurance company, provides the funds to make claim payments for company employees and their dependents.

In the event that claims are higher than predicted, a self-funded health insurance plan can be backed-up by a stop-loss contract. The stop-loss contract is designed to limit your employer's liability for claims.

Generally, there are two variations of this coverage. Specific stop-loss coverage begins to apply after your medical expenses exceed a predetermined threshold such as $5,000. Aggregate stop-loss coverage applies when your employer's liability for group insurance claims exceeds a specified amount. The insurance company will pay all claims once the specified amount is reached.

An employer self-funded plan may be an indemnity program which reimburses you for the medical care you have received. Or, your employer may provide benefits through the service plan offered under an HMO, or through the insurance company's PPO network.

An insurance company may also be used for a self-funded employer to help out with needed administrative services. Under this arrangement, the insurance company will provide claims forms, administer claims, and make payments to health care providers, but the employer will provide the funds to make claims payments.

Self-insurance has four major advantages:

- The company can save money if actual losses are less than those predicted.

- The expense of carrying insurance may be reduced because of the elimination of administrative costs, agent commissions, brokerage fees, and premium tax.

- Because the company has assumed the entire risk, there may be a greater effort on its part to seek ways to reduce claims, and encourage employees to actively participate in "wellness" programs and improved lifestyles.

- The company has use of the money that would normally be held by the insurance company.

The main disadvantages of self-insurance include the following:

- Actual losses may be more than predicted, causing the unexpected loss of funds that were to be used for other purposes.

- Expenses could be higher than expected if additional personnel have to be hired to administer claims, manage risk or offer employee information.

- Income taxes could be higher because the company will not be able to take premiums paid as a deduction. Only the claims paid, and operating expenses may be taken as a tax deduction.

With self-insured health plans, certain federal laws may apply. If a plan is not state regulated, you may want to talk to an attorney specializing in health law before getting involved.

As a rule, partners and sole proprietors are considered self-employed individuals, not employees, so the rules for personally-owned health insurance apply. Government allows anyone who is self-employed to deduct a portion of their health insurance premiums. The deduction was 30 percent for tax years 1994 through 1996. Under new tax laws this deduction will be gradually increased to 80 percent by the year 2002.

If the partnership pays the premiums for medical care insurance on the partners without regard to partnership income, premiums are deductible by the partnership but are included in the partners' taxable income.

Self-insured plans are typically offered by financially strong companies who are able to deposit adequate sums of money to cover employees' medical expenses. Generally employers who install self-insured plans will use the administrative services of an insurer or a third-party administrator (TPA).

Third-party Administrators

A third-party administrator is a firm which provides administrative services for your employer or other associations having group insurance policies. The third-party administrator acts as a liaison between the insurance company and your employer in matters such as certifying eligibility, preparing reports required by the state and processing claims.

The use of third-party administrators became common in the 1990s, as a result of larger employers self-funding health benefits.

Small Employers

Small employers (usually defined as those with fewer than 20-25 employees) have been especially hard hit by increases in health care insurance premiums. Because many group plans are experience rated, small employers see an immediate premium increase whenever claims are particularly high. If the average age of the participants is particularly high, or if claims experience is high, or if there has been even one long or catastrophic illness in a small employer plan, it can have a devastating effect, making health insurance unaffordable for the whole group.

Recent surveys by the Health Insurance Association of America (HIAA) indicate a substantial decline in the number of small firms that are able to offer health coverage to their employees.

Several states have acted to ensure that health insurance coverages are available at a reasonable cost and under reasonable conditions for small employers. Among the new requirements:

- standard benefit plans that must be offered to small employers

- maximum waiting periods for pre-existing conditions

- the insurance company may not exclude particular individuals or medical conditions from coverage

- insurance companies may only cancel small employer plans for nonpayment of premium, fraud, misrepresentation or noncompliance with plan provisions

Cafeteria Plans

With a cafeteria plan, you select health benefits from a variety of options, based on your individual and family needs. Cafeteria plans tend to be more complex (and more expensive) than traditional plans, especially with regard to plan administration, and usually make the most sense for larger employers.

Benefits are elected in advance of the year in which they will be used (benefits to be used in 1996 will be elected at the end of 1995). Taxation of cafeteria plans is regulated by Section 125 of the Internal Revenue Code.

Medical Savings Account

A medical savings account (MSA) is an employer-funded account linked to a high deductible medical indemnity plan. Usually, your employer raises the existing plan deductible (usually by 300 percent to 400 percent) and in turn returns a portion of the premium savings to you as contributions to the medical savings account. You can use these contributions to pay for health care expenses throughout the year, and at the end of the year, you may withdraw whatever remains in the account as (taxable) cash.

Multiple Employer Trusts

Multiple employer trusts provide health insurance benefits to small businesses through a series of trusts usually established based on specific industries such as manufacturing, sales and service, real estate, etc. Most states have group size eligibility requirements for employer groups to qualify for group insurance.

Generally, states may require a minimum of five to ten participants for a group to be eligible for group benefits. METs typically have no such requirements and in reality a group of one could be eligible for group benefits.

METs are formed by insurance companies or third-party administrators who are called sponsors. The sponsor develops the plan, sets the underwriting rules and administers the plan.

To help prevent the possibility of adverse selection, the underwriter must make sure that the sponsor's underwriting rules are adequate and that he or she adheres to them. This is necessary because an employer with only two, three or five employees could elect to join an MET because they know of the poor health condition of one of the employees. The underwriting standards must be able to prevent this from happening.

If state law allows, METs may be noninsured. A noninsured plan is a self-funded plan. It is a plan that operates without the services and funds of an insurance company. The trustee has charge of the funds and the policies and all financial activities occur through the trust.

As with a traditional group insurance plan, a master policy is issued to a trustee who is operating under a trust agreement. The master contract has its own policy effective date and renewal dates which the insurance company may use for changing rates on the MET's entire block of business. Also, every employer under the MET has its own effective dates and anniversary dates. Rates are generally changed on an employer's anniversary date, but usually not more than once a year.

Multiple Employer Welfare Arrangements

Multiple Employer Welfare Arrangements (MEWAs) are employer funds and trusts providing health care benefits (among other benefits) to employees of two or more employers.

ERISA, the federal Employee Retirement Income Security Act which is designed to protect you if you are in a group health insurance plan, restricts states' ability to regulate employee welfare benefit plans while preserving state insurance laws having to do with reserve requirements. A state may regulate insurance, but may or may not consider an employee welfare benefit plan an "insurance plan" for the purpose of regulation.

Some self-funded MEWAs claim they are not subject to Insurance Department regulation and operate under a supposed preemption under ERISA. As a result, many have gone unregulated, and have fraudulently collected premiums from small businesses only to fold and leave millions of dollars of unpaid claims.

Regulators are attempting to resolve the question of jurisdiction. Meanwhile, in most states MEWAs need to obtain a Certificate of Authority in order to transact insurance business, and must be fully insured by a licensed insurance company. Usually, agents and brokers are prohibited from assisting MEWAs to transact insurance until and unless the agent or broker files a report with the Department of Insurance outlining the MEWA's organization, insurance contracts, benefit plan description, and the designated third-party administrator.

Deductible, Co-payment, and Reimbursement

Insured employees with dependent coverage must meet the deductible before expenses will be covered. But, plans typically include some type of family deductible in order to limit a family's exposure for health care expenses.

A family deductible is usually some multiple of the individual deductible, often two or three. For a family deductible to be satisfied, the combined expenses of covered family members are accumulated. Some plans require that at least one family member satisfy the individual deductible before the family deductible can be met.

Co-insurance is a feature typically found in group health plans. It sets the percentage of covered expenses that the employees and the health plan will pay. The most common co-insurance level is one in which the employee pays 20 percent of the expenses and the insurance company pays 80 percent.

A *covered expense* is an eligible expense under a group health insurance plan. It is an expense that will be reimbursed in whole or in part. An example: Most health plans consider doctors' visits a covered expense—that is, any doctor's fee you incur up to the amount provided by your plan.

However, just because an expense is covered does not mean that the coverage is unlimited. Both basic and comprehensive plans have limits on the amount of expenses for which they will reimburse. In addition, you usually have to pay some form of deductible and co-insurance before they will reimburse the expenses.

Insurance companies limit covered expenses in a number of ways. Example: Your insurance company can cap allowable payments for a certain procedure or service (i.e., a surgical schedule). Some insurers also restrict covered expenses by limiting the number of visits or days for home health care or skilled nursing care, or by establishing a reasonable and customary charge.

Dental, Vision, and Prescription Drug Plans

Dental care is usually considered a budgetable expense, so it's usually not included in group health plans. However, you can usually obtain dental care from your employer in the form of employee benefits.

Some health plans do include dental coverage as part of the medical plan. Others include it as a separate add-on plan. Also, many plans do provide coverage for noncosmetic dental work resulting from an accident.

Your employer may also offer direct reimbursement for dental care—this is a noninsured dental coverage plan typically used by smaller employers—in which your employer agrees to pay for a percentage or amount of the expenses. Small employers usually go this route to avoid both the costs associated with an insured plan and the administrative complexity of going through an insurance company. In addition, the risk is considerably smaller because dental expenses, unlike medical expenses, tend to be more predictable and seldom involve catastrophic expenses.

Vision coverage is similar to dental, in that it is a relatively new benefit, usually offered by employers that can afford to add certain fringe benefits typically considered budgetable. Most health plans provide coverage for medical care related to eye injury or disease, but not for costs associated with periodic eye examinations or corrective lenses. Vision care is typically covered on a scheduled basis that pays a fixed dollar amount for examinations, lenses and frames.

Most often, only prescription drugs that are for treatment of an illness or injury are covered by a health plan—subject to applicable deductibles and co-insurance.

Example: Your insurance company might not cover your contraceptive prescription drugs, or the nicotine chewing gum you need to help you quit smoking.

Different insurance companies offer different types of drug plans, but the basic types of prescription medication plans, include open panel, closed panel, mail order and prescription drug card plans.

Summary

Group health insurance dominates the market because it receives a number of critical subsidies from the federal goverment. Most of the subsidies come in the form of tax breaks.

An employer can deduct all premiums paid for group or franchise health insurance on employees as a business expense, provided the employer is not the beneficiary of the policy (benefits are payable to the employees, not the employer). The value of the coverage provided by the employer is not considered taxable income to the employee.

Payments for permanent losses under accidental death and dismemberment coverage (such as loss of a limb or bodily function, loss of sight or hearing, or permanent disfigurement) are not included as taxable income to the employee, regardless of who paid the premium.

Effective in 1997, long-term care insurance provided on a group basis enjoys the same tax status as group life and health insurance, meaning premiums paid by the employer are tax deductible and benefits are received tax free up to specified limits. Medical expense benefits are generally considered to be reimbursements for medical expenses already incurred, and therefore are not taxable as income.

A taxpayer cannot deduct medical expenses from income for tax purposes that have been reimbursed by the insurance company. This is true whether premiums for the policy were paid for by an employer or by the individual.

With all of these tax breaks, it's little wonder that so many people get their health coverage through group policies at work. The only question: Will the federal government ever end the subsidies it gives employers—as part of some larger health insurance reform plan or otherwise?

How Medicare and Medicaid Work

7

How Medicare and Medicaid Work

Medicare is a federal health insurance program for the aged (people 65 and older), people of any age with permanent kidney failure, and certain disabled people. So, if you're one of 38 million Americans who qualify as either aged or disabled, you can get Medicare insurance.

Enrollment can be either automatic or optional—depending on the coverage in question. So, make sure that you filed the right paperwork to get the full package of Medicare coverage.

Technically, Medicare is part of the Social Security System and is administered by the Health Care Financing Administration—an agency of the Department of Health and Human Services. The program is federally funded—which means participants pay very little for the coverage they receive. The coverage applies to hospitalization as well as basic medical expenses.

The basic medical care needed when you are older and covered by Medicare includes, but is not limited to:

- necessary day-to-day outpatient medical care
- occasional hospitalization for care of chronic or acute ailments or accidents
- possibly skilled nursing care in a nursing home

Medicare is designed to provide some benefits for each of these major needs. The benefits aren't great—most private sector health insurance covers more—more completely. But Medicare does offer the functional level of health coverage that most older people in the United States use.

This is a rough outline of Medicare. The practical issues of how the program works can get complicated. Even if you've been in the system for a few years, you may be unclear about what it covers, what it excludes, how much of your medical expenses you will be responsible for, and whether you need additional health insurance.

We'll answer these questions—with as little drudgery as possible.

Limitations Under Medicare

Medicare will pay for some of your health care expenses. It by no means pays for them all. There are limits on covered services—and the program includes both deductibles and co-insurance provisions.

Your doctor often will charge you more for services than Medicare will pay. To fill in these gaps, insurance companies have developed special policies known as Medicare supplement policies.

These policies are profitable. Insurance companies and retiree associations deluge the senior population with ads for Medicare supplement policies. Agents selling Medicare supplements don't always practice the professionalism and ethical conduct they should. Often, the combination of these factors results in poor decision-making with regard to supplemental coverage—buying too much coverage, or the wrong kind, or none at all.

In addition, more direct marketing abuses have occurred. One common scenario: An impresionable older person would end up buying six or seven supplemental policies—when one is all he or she needs. As a result, Medicare supplemental policies are heavily regulated by the government, and consumers have been assured by law of certain important legal rights.

Keep in mind that, even though agents are by law required to exercise great care in recommending and selling Medicare supplement policies, they are paid by commissions on the policies they sell. They may be motivated to sell you higher cost policies than you may not need.

What's Covered Under Medicare?

The first step in determining whether you need a Medicare supplement policy is clearly understanding what types of health care costs are and are not covered by Medicare.

Medicare pays only for services determined to be medically necessary by federal health care experts. Even then the services are covered only to the extent that Medicare determines charges to be reasonable.

Medicare Part A

Medicare is made up of two parts:

- Part A is Hospital Insurance
- Part B is Medical Expense Insurance

Medicare Part A covers costs associated with inpatient care in a hospital and skilled nursing facility care after a hospital stay. It also covers home health care and hospice care. It pays for the cost of whole blood or units of packed cells, after the first three pints during a covered stay in a hospital or skilled nursing facility. In addition, it pays 80 percent of durable medical equipment—such as wheelchairs and walkers—when approved.

Just about every working person will receive Medicare at age 65. Under Part A, any person eligible for Social Security will automatically be eligible for hospital insurance at no charge. You will be automatically enrolled if you're receiving benefits before you reach 65 from either the Railroad Retirement Board or Social Security Administration. Your Medicare card will be mailed to you approximately three months before your reach your 65th birthday and coverage begins on the first day of the month in which you turn 65.

Some Medicare reform efforts have suggested raising the Part A enrollment age to 67, or to some other age. But these reforms remain more speculative than practical.

If you're disabled and receiving benefits from either organization for 24 months, your card will be automatically mailed as well.

However, if you're not receiving retirement benefits, Then you must apply directly to either the Social Security Administration or Railroad Retirement Board. Be sure to do so at least three months before you reach 65, to avoid any delays in coverage. You only have seven months to enroll, beginning three months prior to your 65th birthday. Otherwise, you'll have to wait until January 1 though March 31 just to enroll. In that case, your benefits don't kick in until July 1. So, be sure you know your dates.

You are also eligible for benefits if you are one of the following:

- a disabled person who has been receiving Social Security disability benefits for at least 24 months
- a person who is diagnosed as having permanent kidney failure which requires dialysis or a kidney transplant
- an individual born prior to 1909 who has no quarters of coverage under Social Security
- a retired railroad worker

Furthermore, if you don't qualify for Medicare hospital insurance (you don't have the required work credits, etc.), you can buy coverage for a monthly premium. In the mid-1990s, the monthly premium was around $200. If you plan to take this route, you must also enroll in Part B Medicare, be a resident of the United States and either a citizen or a lawfully admitted alien.

Still Working?

If you decide to continue to work after the age of 65, you will still be covered by Medicare. However, such coverage will—in most cases—be secondary to other insurance.

Example: If a company has at least 20 employees, employees over 65 must be offered the same health benefits as younger employees. Medicare becomes a secondary payor of benefits for the employees over 65. The company's health plan is primary.

Accordingly, any health claim made by an age 65 or older employee will first be paid by the group health insurance. If any part of the claim is not satisfied by the company's plan, that portion of the claim would then be submitted to Medicare.

An important note: You may reject your employer's plan and elect Medicare as the primary payor, but your employer may not—in any way—encourage you to make Medicare your primary coverage.

Common tactics employers use to subtly encourage the decision: offering to pay for Part B coverage on your behalf and offering to purchase a Medicare supplement policy for you.

Medicare also becomes the secondary insurer in cases where medical care is to be provided under the provisions of a liability policy, including an automobile policy.

How Much Does It Cost?

If you or your spouse worked for at least 10 years in a Medicare covered job (meaning you were having deductions withheld from your paycheck for payroll withholding tax) and you are a citizen or permanent resident of the United States and eligible for Medicare, there is no charge for Part A (Hospital Insurance). Disabled individuals, kidney dialysis and certain transplant patients are not charged either.

If none of these fit your particular circumstances, you may purchase Medicare Part A if you are at least 65 years of age and meet other restrictions. The per-month cost in 1997 (based on 30 to 40 quarters of Medicare-qualifying employment) was $187. If you worked fewer than 30 quarters during your adult life, the monthly cost was $311.

There is, however, a fee for Part B (Medical Expenses). In 1997, the monthly premium was $43.80 and automatically deducted from Social Security payments. Enrollment is automatic—unless you state you don't want it—when you are eligible for premium-free Part A. If you don't qualify for premium-free Part A, but are 65 or older, you can still buy Part B.

Medicare claims are usually paid on a reimbursement basis, meaning directly to you, the patient—usually after you've already paid the doctor. Benefit payments may also be made directly to a participating provider. Participating health care providers are certified and approved by Medicare for payment of benefits and have agreed to accept the amount reimbursed by Medicare as payment in full.

This kind of agreement is important, because hospital insurance can help pay for inpatient hospital care, inpatient care in a skilled nursing facility, home health care, and hospice care.

For this part of Medicare coverage, you will have to pay a deductible of $760 for each benefit period, beginning with the first day of admission to a hospital and continuing for 60 days. If you are released or hospitalized for more than 60 days, a new benefit period begins and a new deductible applies. That's the bad news. The good news is: There is no limit on the number of benefit periods you can have.

What Part A Does Not Cover

Hospital insurance under Medicare does not cover the following:

- private duty nursing
- charges for a private room, unless medically necessary
- conveniences, such as a telephone or television in your room
- the first three pints of blood received during a calendar year (unless replaced by a blood plan)

Medicare Part B

Medicare Part B is Medical Expense insurance covering costs associated with doctors' services, outpatient care, laboratory tests, x-rays, mammograms and pap smears, and medical supplies. You'll have to pay the first $100, which is the annual deductible, then Medicare will pay 80 percent of all approved charges for any eligible medical expense. The approved charge may or may not be close to the actual fee charged by your provider, and you are responsible for the difference, as well as the additional 20 percent of the approved charge.

Fortunately, when doctors accept a Medicare assignment, they agree to charge no more than Medicare's approved charge.

Here's what Part B covers:

- doctors services provided on an inpatient or outpatient basis, no matter where received in the United States, and including surgical services, diagnostic tests and x-rays, medical supplies furnished in a doctor's office, and services of the office nurse

- services of clinical psychologists, chiropractors, podiatrists and optometrists
- outpatient diagnostic services and medical lab fees, such as care in an emergency room or outpatient clinic of a hospital
- outpatient physical and speech therapy
- certified nurse-midwife services for pregnancies (of course, this benefit isn't used much by those over 65)
- dental work which is required due to accident or disease
- the use of outpatient medical equipment such as iron lungs, braces, colostomy bags, and prosthetic devices such as artificial heart valves
- ambulance service, if the patient's condition requires it
- outpatient psychiatric care (there is a 50 percent co-payment instead of 20 percent)
- the cost of certain vaccines and antigens. (Only medicines which are administered at the hospital or at a doctor's office are covered by Medicare. Drugs which can be self-administered—taken at home—are not covered, even if prescribed by a doctor.)
- an unlimited number of home health care visits, if all required conditions are met and you do not have Medicare hospital (Part A) coverage
- preventive health care expenses such as pap smears and mammography (however, mammograms are covered only when performed in a Medicare-approved facility)
- one pair of eyeglasses following cataract surgery

Blood is a covered expense under Part B (also Part A). In essence, there is a "3-pint deductible" for blood, which means that you are responsible for either paying for the first 3 pints of blood or replacing the blood. The blood deductible for Part B can be used to satisfy the blood deductible for Part A. Thus, only one 3-pint deductible is required. However, any blood provided under Part B is still subject to the 20 percent co-payment.

Under Part B, there are a number of services that do not require a deductible or a co-payment, including:

- the cost of a second opinion required by Medicare for surgery
- home health services (except the 20 percent co-payment applies to the use of certain medical equipment)
- pneumococcal vaccine (flu shots)
- outpatient clinical diagnostic lab tests conducted by Medicare-certified facilities or doctors who accept assignments

Medicare Supplements

Even with Part A and B coverage, the financial risks related to deductibles and co-payments can be financially overwhelming for a retiree living on a modest fixed income. This is particularly true should you develop a major chronic ailment and have to come up with tens of thousands of dollars out of your own pocket.

Medicare is not going to pick up the tab for all of your healthcare needs. The government estimates that Medicare really only pays about half of the costs needed to cover the elderly and there are large gaps in coverage. For instance, Medicare doesn't cover the cost of hearing aids or eye glasses, items virtually essential to seniors today.

As a consequence, insurance companies stepped in to fill those gaps in coverage. Approximately 89 percent of all Medicare recipients supplement their coverage with what are commonly referred to as Medicare Supplement policies or "Medigap" insurance.

The *Omnibus Budget Reconciliation Act of 1990 (OBRA 1990)* enhanced other protections for Medicare supplement consumers. Under this law, Medicare supplement insurance may not be denied on the basis of the senior citizen's health status, claims experience, or medical condition during the first six months a Medicare beneficiary age 65 or older first enrolls in Part B of Medicare. This is known as the open enrollment requirement. During this period, you may purchase a Medicare supplement policy without providing a proof of insurability. After this period of time, evidence of insurability will have to be provided.

To clarify benefits and standardize the types of policies offered, Congress passed a law effective August 1, 1992, directing all insurance companies to standardize the policies they offer as Medicare Supplements. As a result, 10 standard plans were developed by the National Association of Insurance Commissioners (NAIC) and are the only plans that may be sold as Medicare Supplement policies.

The best part is that you can't be turned down, for any reason, as long as you're 65 and apply within six months after you first enroll in Medicare Part B. The policies are guaranteed renewable, meaning you have the right to renew the policy with no change in terms, as long as you pay the premium. The only catch is your insurance company can—and often does—increase your premium when claims costs exceed premium revenue.

Medicare Supplement policies have letter designations, corresponding to the level of benefits provided, beginning with the basic plan labeled "A" and progressively increasing in benefits to the most comprehensive plan labeled "J."

Each state must allow companies to sell Plan A and all Medigap companies must make Plan A available if they sell the more extensive and expensive plans. However, companies are not required to make all 10 plans available. They can sell just a few—as long as Plan A is one of them.

The policies are designed specifically to work with Medicare, to provide supplemental accident and sickness insurance for hospital, medical or surgical expenses. Most, if not all, pick up Medicare's co-insurance charge to you—and may even pay your deductible.

Many charges not covered by Medicare, such as prescription drugs for outpatients, are included in some of the plans. (However, coverage for prescription drug costs may be subject to an annual limit.) The more comprehensive plans also cover the co-payment required for hospital and skilled nursing facility stays. They also cover the 20 percent of approved charges you would ordinarily pay under Part B of Medicare.

What's Included?

You can think of buying Medicare supplement coverage like buying a car. The core benefits represent the basic sticker price of the vehicle. You can add optional benefits to the core package in much the same way that you can add options to the car. The optional benefits included depend on the needs and wants of the individual.

Basic Benefits (Plan A) supplement Medicare benefits by providing coverage for your hospitalization co-insurance payment from day 61-90 and 91-150. This means that the $190 and $380 per day you would be required to pay under Medicare, will be paid for by the supplement. If your benefits end during a period of hospitalization, the supplement pays for an additional 365 days at 100 percent.

In addition, the 20 and 50 percent co-insurance payment under Medicare Part B is covered after you pay the required $100 deductible. The first three pints of blood or packed red blood cells are covered as well under both Part A and B.

Plan B includes the Basic Benefits and adds on coverage for the Medicare Part A deductible of $760 per benefit period. Therefore, if you had Plan B, you would have met your deductible and all co-insurance payments.

Plan C includes everything in Plan A and B and adds the co-insurance amount of $95 a day for skilled nursing care you would be required to pay under Medicare Part A for days 21-100. It pays the $100 deductible under Medicare Part B and 80 percent of emergency care while in a foreign country after a $250 deductible. If you travel out of the country, you may want to consider this!

Plan D includes everything preceding it except the Medicare Part B deductible and adds on coverage for custodial care (dressing, laundry, shopping, etc.). Medicare Part A Home Health Care coverage does not pay for custodial care and many seniors need assistance with daily life functions, especially after recovering from a serious illness or injury. This pays up to $1600 a year for short-term assistance.

Plan E does not cover the Medicare Part B deductible or At-Home Recovery services but does include Preventive Care. The benefit amount is $120 per year for routine physical exams, screening procedures such as blood pressure and cholesterol as well as patient education.

Plan F does not include Preventive Care or At-Home recovery but does add on Excess Charges for Medicare Part B expenses. What this means is if you go to a doctor that does not accept Medicare assignments (meaning they will not honor the Medicare approved charges), you would be obligated to pay the entire bill. This benefit pays the amount you'll be billed for at either 100 percent or 80 percent. If 80 percent, you would be obligated to pay the remaining 20 percent.

Plan G excludes the Medicare Part B deductible and Preventive Care and pays the Excess Charges at a level of 80 percent, rather than 100 percent as in Plan F.

Plan H includes coverage for prescription medications at 50 percent with an annual limit of $1,250 per year, after a $250 deductible is met. This is called the Basic Benefit. An Extended Benefit is available only in Plan J that increases the annual amount to $3,000.

Plan I excludes Medicare Part B deductible and Preventive Care but includes Prescription Drugs at the basic level of $1,250 annually.

Plan J is the most comprehensive and includes coverage for all benefits previously listed at the maximum levels. It is also the most costly, however.

Which one of these plans should you buy? Plan A generally absorbs most of the potential expenses not covered by Medicare—with the exception of the nursing home co-payments. So, many people would have enough coverage if they bought Plan A. However, data from the federal government show that Plan F is the most commonly purchased.

While the benefits will be the same, no matter what company issues the policy, prices will vary from state to state and company to company. That's because not all states have the same medical costs and insurance companies have different claims experience.

During the 1980s and 1990s, Medigap prices increased steadily. This forced many people—and companies—to opt for a managed care approach to cover seniors' health care issues.

Since Plan C is Plan C, no matter which company is offering it, when you shop around for coverage, you'll be looking at price, service and reliability. It's also vital to find an insurance company you feel comfortable with—and one that is reputable and in good shape financially. Your state insurance department can alert you to any problem companies.

A major caveat: You only need one Medicare supplement policy, because only one policy will pay benefits. Although it is unethical and illegal to duplicate existing coverage for the sake of generating a premium and commission, agents have been known to do so.

There are serious penalties for agents who duplicate or "pile on" supplemental coverage, including the loss of their license to sell insurance, jail terms for up to two years, and fines of up to $10,000.

Preexisting Conditions

Many older people are being treated for some medical problems. These conditions may be significant (high blood pressure, heart conditions, etc.) or minor (such as allergies or mild hearing loss). In any event, for insurance purposes these problems are defined as preexisting conditions.

As with any health insurance policy, you should investigate the coverage limitations for preexisting conditions. First, read through the policy and ask your agent for an explanation. Most Medicare supplement contracts define a preexisting condition as any condition for which the policyholder sought treatment or advice in the six months prior to the effective date of the policy.

Most Medicare supplements have a six month waiting period for coverage of preexisting conditions. Some companies have no preexisting condition exclusion, some impose a 90-day or three month exclusion, but none can be greater than six months.

Choosing a Doctor

About half of the doctors in the country will accept the amounts paid by Medicare as payment in full. This is referred to as accepting the Medicare assignment. As an example, if a pathologist or radiologist who performs services on an inpatient basis will accept a Medicare assignment, Medicare will pay 100 percent of reasonable charges. Medicare will also pay the cost of a Medicare-required second opinion for surgery with no 20 percent co-payment. Medicare will also pay for services of other specialists on the same 80 percent of reasonable charges basis.

Doctors who do not accept Medicare assignments are prohibited by law from charging more than 140 percent of the Medicare prevailing charge for office and hospital visits. For other services, such as surgery, the limit is 125 percent.

In the past, some doctors have tried to circumvent these limiting charges by requiring patients to contract to pay full charges. The Health Care Financing Administration has cautioned that these contracts are not valid.

Doctors, suppliers and other providers must submit claims for covered Part B services directly to Medicare, regardless of whether they are a participating or a nonparticipating provider. Some doctors ask patients to waive the right to have doctors submit Medicare claims, and obligate the patient to pay privately for Medicare-covered services. These waivers are also invalid, according to the HCFA, and could subject physicians to civil penalties.

If your doctor has not accepted your Medicare assignment, he will send the bill for Part A services directly to you. In turn, you fill out a Medicare claim form and attach any itemized bills from your doctor —including date of treatment, place of treatment, description of treatment, doctor's name and charge for service. The documents are then sent to the Medicare adminstrator in your area. Upon receiving the claim, the administrator will send an Explanation of Medicare Benefits, showing which services are covered and the amounts approved for each service.

Appealing Your Claim

If your Medicare claims are denied, you are probably going to want to appeal your claim. Within six months of receiving the Explanation of Medicare Benefits notice, you must file a written request for review. The administrator will check for miscalculations or other clerical errors. If the administrator declines to make a change, an appeal can be made to the Social Security office (but only if the amount disputed is $100 or more).

You must appear in person to attend a hearing and present evidence, such as a doctor's letter, to support your point. A written notice of the decision will be sent to you after the hearing.

Medicare HMOs

Due to the increasing costs of Medicare Supplement policies, many seniors are switching to managed care plans. In 1998, the federal government estimated that some 70,000 Medicare recipients a month were switching to some form of managed care. At that point, of the 38 million seniors and disabled eligible for Medicare, almost 6 million were enrolled in a Medicare HMO.

Medicare HMOs combine the benefits of Medicare and Medigap policies all in one. However, some participants have complained about the non-responsiveness that the plans share with other managed care programs.

The federal government funds most of the revenue for each participating HMO, which makes the cost to you about the same as the premium you would normally pay for Medicare Part B, depending upon the HMO. (However, that may be changing soon, with rising costs and increased claims, companies are beginning to charge premiums in addition to the government's funding.)

Items such as eyeglasses and prescription drugs are covered under most HMOs. As long as you have Medicare Part B, continue to make the payments and live in a service plan's area, you are eligible for enrollment without health screening.

You can find the names of HMO plans in your area by calling your state's insurance office. Remember, however, the same criticisms previously discussed in terms of HMOs still apply.

Once you enroll in a Medicare HMO, you can switch back to Medicare anytime. However, you may not switch back to a Medicare Supplement policy you previously had without the company's permission. And, you can be sure it will review your health record if you do and possibly turn you down. That's why some seniors hang on to their Medicare Supplement policy while enrolled in an HMO. This assures continuous coverage under the supplement if they change their minds and go back to traditional Medicare service.

The other managed care option you have is through a program called Medicare Select. Basically, this is another form of Medicare supplement insurance sponsored by the federal government, that may or may not be continued. In 1998, Medicare Select came up for review and—by the end of 1998—the Medicare system still was having trouble replacing it as a Medicare option.

Congress proposed Medicare Select in 1990 as a pilot program for those seniors who wanted some level of choice in where and with whom they could secure health services. Service delivery is in the form of a Preferred Provider Organization (PPO) and provides standard Medicare supplement benefits, depending on which policy you buy.

If you buy a Medicare Select policy, you are buying one of the standard Medicare Supplement policies. You can purchase a policy through an insurance company or HMO—but be sure to inquire which policy you are buying. When you enroll in a Medicare Select policy (should such policies continue to be available), you choose a physician or medical provider from a list provided by the insurance company of "preferred providers." To receive full benefits you must go to the doctor or medical provider selected.

If you choose to go elsewhere, Medicare Select policies are not required to pay any benefits for non-emergency services. So, it pays to go to your doctor of choice. And, if you decide you don't like the policy, you can always return to an individual Medicare policy. You will, however, have to reapply for a Medicare Supplement—just as with HMOs.

The Last Resort: Medicaid

If insurance companies consider you uninsurable—because of your age or a pre-existing condition—you probably can obtain coverage for a state-sponsored health insurance program.

State-sponsored programs should be used as a last resort, because they typically offer only limited benefits, are expensive and usually include a waiting period before your coverage kicks in. But at least they're there, if you need them. You can find out about these plans by calling your state insurance department.

Medicaid provides medical assistance to low-income families and individuals of all ages. The program works well for seniors who have run through most of their assets. In fact, The Health Care Finance Administration reports that about half of all Medicaid spending goes to people who had financial resources when they entered a nursing home, but reached the poverty level while they were there. A third of the $55-billion-a-year budget for Medicaid goes to those over 65, primarily to support them in nursing homes.

What Services Are Covered Under Medicaid?

Medicaid offers a minimum set of services including hospital, physician, and nursing home services. Additionally, state agencies have the option of covering an additional 31 services including prescription drugs, hospice care and personal care services.

Medicaid is the largest insurer of long-term care (LTC) in the United States—covering the bulk of what most people would consider the middle class. It covers 68 percent of nursing home residents and over 50 percent of nursing home costs.

In 1995, Medicaid expenditures for health care amounted to $152 billion. States paid $66 billion (43 percent) and the Feds paid $86 billion (57 percent). Using up a lifetime of assets is a frightening scenario for an older person on his or her own. But what if your spouse is still living at home and you must move into a nursing home? Will you have to sell the house to cover your nursing home costs? Where will your spouse live?

At one time, Medicaid rules did require you to liquidate virtually all of your assets—including cash, investments (such as stocks and bonds), bank accounts, real estate and even some forms of cash-value life insurance—to qualify for coverage. Fortunately, the federal government modified the requirements in 1993 to allow surviving spouses and disabled children to retain more of the family's assets.

Now, if you are married and you enter a nursing home while your spouse remains in your house, the at-home spouse is permitted to keep the following:

- one home
- one car
- the greater of one-half of the couple's assets or $75,740
- up to $1,919 in monthly income

These amounts are indexed annually for inflation and are significantly lower for unmarried seniors. However, once neither spouse is living in or likely to return to the home and the house is sold, Medicaid may demand reimbursement for expenses associated with prior nursing home services.

An entire "Medicaid Planning" specialty has emerged in the estate planning field to help people avoid running through their life savings before qualifying for Medicaid. Some people are even tempted to give away assets so that they can qualify for Medicaid and still pass something along to their heirs. However, the government frowns on this: Federal provisions enacted in 1996 set criminal penalties for transferring assets for the sole purpose of qualifying for

Medicaid. The penalties include fines of up to $25,000 and imprisonment for up to five years.

Summary

Medicare and Medicaid aren't the only government programs that provide subsidized health insurance to Americans. The federal government offers smaller programs directed at focused groups, and state governments usually offer their own versions of subsidized health care for poor people. But Medicare and Medicaid are the main programs in the government system. Understanding their mechanics should help you navigate similar terrain. And "navigating" is the right word. Whatever government agency runs them, these programs are full of intricate details that can make claims tough to file.

Counseling services may be available in your state to provide advice concerning the purchase of Medicare supplement insurance and concerning Medicaid.

This chapter has considered the basic mechanics of the main government health insurance programs. It should give you a functional understanding of how to move through them effectively.

Workers' Compensation

Workers' Compensation 8

So far, we have concentrated upon how the various types of personal health care coverage work. Outside of—or in addition to—those types of coverage is a health care financing mechanism that comes from the corporate world: *workers' compensation.*

Workers' comp programs are designed to provide a satisfactory means of handling occupational injuries and disabilities. As a consumer, you'll probably never buy a workers' comp policy, but you may care a lot about how the system works if you're ever hurt on the job.

In terms of dollars of claims paid each year, workers' comp systems account for more health care than indemnity plans, managed care plans or Medicare.

Workers' comp is administrered on the state level. And every state requires employers to provide some form of workers' comp benefits for their employees. Some history helps explain why the programs are so important.

The industrial revolution gave birth to new industries and brought together great numbers of employees: unskilled, undisciplined—and often selected without regard to character. Workers were exposed to hazards not in existence before, such as rapidly moving power belts, moving machine parts, hot or molten metals, poisonous gases and chemicals.

More often than not, workers toiled in places that were poorly lighted and ventilated. Labor was plentiful, wages were low, and workers were exhausted from long hours on the job.

Industrial development proceeded rapidly, though at the expense of the workers. An industrial accident could leave a worker injured with little or no recourse in response to injuries or lost wages. During the 19th Century, if you were injured on the job you only had one source of redress against your employer: Institute a suit under common law.

There were no written laws or statutes with regards to the employer/employee relationship. Common law cases favored the employer—the only way you could recover money for injuries was to prove that the injuries were due to your employer's negligence.

Negligence was defined as "the lack of that degree of care that a person of ordinary prudence would exercise under like or similar circumstances." In this case, person refers to employers—but it's a good idea to keep in mind, generally.

When an injured employee could establish that injuries were the result of the employer's negligence, damages could be recovered. However, the common law in existence during this time allowed the employer three defenses against negligence suits brought by employees for injuries sustained in the course of employment. The three common law defenses were:

- assumption of risk
- contributory negligence
- fellow-servant rule

The assumption of risk defense stated that an employer could not be held liable for injury to an employee who voluntarily enters into the employment, knowing about any unsafe conditions of the premises or work, and who understands the risks likely to accompany the employment.

The contributory negligence defense held that even if the employer violated his duty to provide a safe workplace and was negligent, the injured employee was not entitled to recover damages if the employee's own negligence had contributed to the injuries.

The contributory negligence concept evolved into comparative negligence, or consideration given to the extent to which each party's negligence contributed to the injury. That remains a big employment issue today.

The third principle, the fellow-servant rule, stated that an employer was not liable for an injury to an employee injured solely as a result of the negligence of a fellow servant (that is, a fellow employee), who was acting within the scope of his or her employment. This was an often-used argument.

Needless to say, getting your employer to pay during the industrial revolution wasn't exactly a piece of cake. This inability increased the number of industrial injuries and diseases and resulted in a large number of uncompensated workers and their families. Eventually, this began to pose serious social problems and impact the nation's economic health.

Today, with the enactment of workers' comp laws, things are done somewhat differently. Now, the law holds that the employer shall assume the costs for benefits that the law says the employee is owed.

You—the employee—pay nothing for this protection. Your employer includes the cost of workers' comp benefits in the price charged for products or services just as he includes other operating costs—such as salaries, rent, telephone expenses, supplies and other operating and production expenses.

This coverage isn't completely free. In most situations, employees have given up their right to file suit against employers for workplace injuries in exchange for the benefits. Some classes of employees are exempt from the laws, and suits may still be filed for damages which are not covered by the compensation law. In those cases which do fall outside the law, the three common law defenses are still available to the employers.

The workers' compensation system benefits both you and your employer. Even though your employer loses the right to defend himself in cases where he may not have been negligent, he can predict the costs necessary for employee injuries by means of his workers' compensation insurance premium. In most states, he can even reduce the insurance premium by reducing losses through implementing a safety program.

Through the 1980s and 1990s, however, the cost of workers' comp exploded. In 1991, the system cost employers $70 billion—that's almost twice what they paid in 1985. The impact was even wider than the 1986-to-1991 statistics suggest. The cost of the average workers' comp claim more than tripled in ten years, passing the $20,000 mark.

While all state systems have the same objective—to provide benefits to workers injured without question as to fault—the similarity ends there. State laws differ not only in detail, but in almost every major feature. So, it's important that you look into the features that make up your state laws, and determine how the program is administered in your state.

Eligibility

It is important to distinguish between the eligibility requirements for health insurance and those for workers' comp insurance. With a health insurance policy, the employer may decide to offer coverage only to a class of employees, such as "all salaried employees" or "employees who have worked one year or more for the firm."

With workers' comp insurance, singling out classes of employees for coverage is not permitted. Eligibility for workers' comp is statutorily determined. Unless exempted as described above, by law, full-time employees, part-time employees—and even illegal workers are covered by workers' comp insurance in California.

In order to be eligible for workers' comp benefits you must work in an occupation that is covered by workers' comp and have had an accident or sickness that is work-related.

In most states, all workers (except those specifically excluded or exempted) come under workers' comp laws. For these states, the law must list the employees excluded. Commonly excluded employee include:

- farm labor
- domestic servants
- casual workers

Even for these employees, workers' comp coverage is usually available on a voluntary basis at the election of the employer.

Early workers' compensation laws applied only to very hazardous occupations. Over the years, the scope of the laws has expanded to embrace more and more occupational groups. Every state has some exempt classifications, but it is estimated that about 90 percent of the nation's employees now fall under workers' compensation laws.

Some states exempt employers from workers' comp laws if they employ fewer than a stipulated number of employees (usually three). But, even if an employer has fewer than three employees, he may voluntarily decide to comply with the workers' comp law to avoid liability claims down the road.

Today, in most states, an employer subject to compensation laws is obligated to buy workers' comp insurance or demonstrate an ability to provide the required benefits. However, most states permit an employer to set up a formal program of self-insurance—including specific loss-handling procedures and proper funding of reserves against claims. Companies large enough to offer self-funded health insurance to employees are usually good bets to self-insure their workers' comp.

The purpose of workers' comp is to provide you with benefits if you have an accident or sickness that is job-related—arising out of and in the course of employment. Falling on the dance floor while attempting the Electric Slide and breaking your arm does not make a workers' comp claim—slipping on a wet floor at the job site and breaking your arm does.

Benefits

Workers' comp laws provide for the payment of four types of benefits:

- medical benefits
- income benefits
- death benefits
- rehabilitation benefits

For the purposes of this book, we will focus on the medical and rehabilitation portions of workers' comp benefits. The others do not directly impact health coverage issues.

Medical benefits provided under workers' comp are, simply, unlimited. If you have an injury or disease, you are entitled to receive all necessary medical and surgical treatment to cure or relieve the condition.

Certain maximums or limits may apply to a type of care or a particular medical item—for example, stress-related psychotherapy may be limited to a specific number of visits—but overall benefits are unlimited.

Rehabilitaiton benefits have become recognized as a valuable tool for reducing workers' comp costs and returning disabled employees to their jobs, as soon as possible. These benefits cover physical therapy, alternative-medicine treatment and related treatment that does not necessarily fit in a strict definition of medical service.

Rehabilitation benefits under a workers' comp policy will usually provide coverage for services such as therapy, vocational training, devices such as wheelchairs, and certain costs connected with travel, lodging and living expenses while you are being rehabilitated.

Rehabilitation also aids the insurance company. It helps to restore the injured worker to his former earning capacity. Today, insurance companies are among the leaders in providing rehabilitation for the industrially injured.

Most states offer rehabilitation benefits. Some states have set up a special fund to provide these benefits, while others have not. Various states impose weekly limits, maximum limits and special limits for specific types of rehabilitation. The laws—and the benefits provided—vary somewhat from state to state. But benefits tend to be low—about $300 a week at the most.

If you are seriously injured, you might need to see a specialist for follow-up care. These costs are typically covered by your employer under workers' compensation benefits. However, your employer might have a say in deciding what specialist you see.

What Does Workers' Comp Cover?

As mentioned before, workers' compensation coverage applies to bodily injuries and diseases "arising out of and in the course of employment." Covered losses must be work-related (losses that are non-work-related are not covered by workers' compensation).

Only occupational diseases unique to the occupation are covered. A cause-and-effect relationship must exist between the job and the disease, and ordinary diseases suffered by the general public are not covered.

The laws commonly require that higher benefits be paid for certain losses as a penalty to the employer. Benefits are often increased if a loss results from the

> Any *covered injury* must be accidental, and that term includes death resulting from the accident.

serious or willful misconduct of the employer (for example, failing to provide required safety equipment). A number of states require that double benefits be paid for injury to a minor who is employed illegally. These extra payments are not covered by a workers' compensation policy, and the additional amount must be borne by the employer.

The cumulative effect of two injuries combined can be greater than the effect of the same two injuries in isolation. Example: An employee who loses sight in one eye would still be able to function in many jobs. If that employee suffered a subsequent injury causing loss of sight in the other eye, the disability would be greater than if the first injury had not occurred.

Once a person has been incapacitated, there is a greater risk that an additional injury may lead to permanent total disability, requiring higher statutory benefits than might be expected for the second injury alone.

Policy Endorsements

When the first workers' compensation laws were passed, there were no insurance companies providing workers' comp coverage. Companies paid benefits out of operating funds.

Today, many property and casualty insurance companies offer workers' comp insurance, while some companies specialize only in workers' compensation insurance.

Six states have passed laws requiring that any workers' comp insurance purchased in that state must be purchased from a fund set up by the state and not from a private insurance company. When such arrangements exist, they are called "monopolistic state funds" or "exclusive funds." The six states are Nevada, North Dakota, Ohio, Washington, West Virginia, and Wyoming.

In other states, there is no state workers' compensation fund—insurance must be purchased from private insurance companies. And in some states, both a state fund and private insurance companies compete for business from employers.

Insurers are not obligated to use any particular workers' comp policy form, and some variations may be found in the contract actually being issued. However, the National Council on Compensation Insurance has developed a standard policy, and it is followed with a degree of uniformity.

The standard policy provides a complete package of protection for an employer's obligations under workers' comp law and liability which is outside that law. Endorsements may be used to cover exposures which are not insured by the basic policy.

Policy Components

In its current form, the policy has eight parts:

- Information page (or Declarations page)
- General section
- Part I—Workers' compensation
- Part II—Employers' liability
- Part III—Other states insurance
- Part IV—Duties if injury occurs
- Part V—Premium
- Part VI—Conditions

The policy includes two coverage parts. Part I, workers' comp, protects the policyholder against statutory claims. Part II, employers' liability, protects against common law claims. Some common provisions are repeated in each section.

Under each coverage, the insurance applies to accidental bodily injury, death or disease, occurring during the policy period and caused or aggravated by the conditions of employment by the insured.

In short, workers' comp is first-dollar coverage. You don't have to worry about deductibles or co-insurance. You don't have to worry about limits to coverage, etc. If you are injured at work, you will be covered for whatever medical care you need to get better. The only issues that will impact your treatment are related to seeing the doctor that your employer suggests (and even those are limited).

Supplementary payments are also provided, including coverage for appeal bonds, bonds to release attachments, interest on judgments, claim expenses, litigation costs taxed against the employer and certain other expenses (other than loss of earnings) incurred at the insurance company's request.

Under workers' comp, your employer has subrogation rights if anyone other than you is liable for a covered injury. Subrogation is designed to prevent a company from collecting twice for the same loss. It only applies when a third party caused the loss or was primarily responsible for it through negligence.

If any other insurance applies, the insurance company will only pay its share of claims and costs—subject to any limits of liability, all shares will be equal until a loss is paid. (Note: in contrast to most other forms of commercial casualty insurance, workers' compensation and employers' liability coverage contribute equal shares when other insurance applies. Most other coverages contribute proportionally based upon the respective limits of insurance.)

Coverage Issues

Certain payments will be the sole responsibility of your employer and not the insurance company. Any required payments which are in excess of the benefits regularly provided

> Penalties may also be imposed for discharging, coercing, or discriminating against an employee.

by the law are not covered by the policy. Such penalties may be required if you employer is guilty of serious or willful misconduct, or knowingly employs someone in violation of law, or fails to comply with health and safety regulations.

Some general statutory provisions will apply automatically. These provisions declare that the insurance company and your employer are one and the same with regard to notice of injury given by a worker, and with respect to matters of legal jurisdiction. Bankruptcy of the employer will not relieve the insurance company of its policy obligations. The insurance company agrees to be directly and primarily liable to anyone entitled to insurance benefits.

The policy says that the insurance conforms to the workers' compensation law, and any policy provisions in conflict with the law are automatically changed to conform with it.

Employers' Liability

The limits of employers' liability include bodily injury by accident, bodily disease and bodily disease by aggregate. This coverage protects against a variety of common law exposures. It is needed to fill gaps in the compensation coverage and to cover claims not subject to the compensation laws.

Although you—as an employee—give up the right to sue in exchange for workers' comp benefits, not all employees come under the law. Those not covered may sue.

In recent years, successful suits against employers have also been filed by spouses and children of injured workers. Employers' liability insurance covers these claims.

Under Employers' Liability coverage, the insurance company agrees to pay all sums (subject to policy limits) which your employer becomes legally obligated to pay as damages because of employee injuries which are covered by the insurance—providing that damages result directly from an injury arising out of and in the course of employment.

Employers' Liability Coverage covers the following types of claims:

- damages claimed by a third party
- care and loss of service
- consequential injury to a spouse or relative of the injured worker
- actions brought against the insured in a capacity other than as employer

Injuries to workers covered by federal laws—for example, the Longshoreman's Act—are excluded because the policy is designed to cover exposures which are subject to state jurisdiction, but coverage for many of these exposures may be added to a policy by endorsement. Fines, penalties and damages for violations of law are excluded because the policy is designed to cover only the actual legal liability exposures of employers.

Occupational Diseases

Since many occupational diseases—such as asbestosis, silicosis and diseases associated with radiation exposure—are slow to develop, several administrative problems can result:

- a worker may be employed by several employers and be under a constant disease exposure
- the disability may take place sometime after the last injurious exposure
- due to the time period involved, several different carriers may cover workers' comp for the same employer

Because workers' comp only provides on-the-job coverage, it does not provide coverage after work hours, or on weekends, holidays or vacations.

Traditionally, other forms of health insurance have provided non-occupational coverage only, for injuries and diseases which are not work-related. Many of these policies contain a workers' comp exclusion. Coverage is specifically excluded for losses which are covered by workers' comp laws, disability benefit laws or similar laws.

Many people have both occupational and non-occupational coverage because employers frequently provide or make group health insurance available. Others purchase individual or family plans of health insurance for non-occupational exposures. But this division of coverage means that separate insurance policies and separate insurance carriers are involved, that there is a need to determine whether each claim is work-related or not, and that some gaps in coverage or duplications of coverage may exist.

24-Hour Coverage

There have been several proposals aimed at 24-hour coverage—a blend of occupational and non-occupational coverage into a single coverage package, or at least provide a single delivery system or administrative system. Various proposals accomplish this goal to different degrees.

The proponents of 24-hour coverage maintain that the concept offers a number of potential advantages. Most of these relate to possible cost savings, but a few lie in the coverage area.

The most significant advantages which have been identified are:

- possible reductions in gaps in coverage, which would be advantageous to companies
- possible reductions in duplications of coverage for the same loss, which would reduce insurance costs
- possible administrative savings resulting from combining the claims processing systems
- possible structural efficiencies and savings resulting from integrating different health care delivery systems

Although it is generally understood that 24-hour coverage means some combination of occupational and non-occupational forms of health insurance, there is no single definition of what 24-hour coverage means or what it should include. With this approach, 24-hour disability coverage is offered in a single policy that includes limited medical benefits.

In this case, disability benefits are provided for all of an employee's injuries or diseases, whether work-related or not, but medical benefits are provided only for work-related injuries and diseases.

Example: John has 24-hour disability coverage and is injured in his backyard when he falls off a ladder while painting his house. John has emergency medical treatment, a period of hospital confinement, and is unable to work for two months. This policy will pay disability income benefits to John, but will not pay any of his medical expenses (because the injury was not work-related).

Accident Coverage

Accident coverage would provide 24-hour medical and disability coverage for all accidental injuries, whether work-related or not, but only work-related diseases would be covered. Here, we find broad accident coverage and limited coverage for diseases.

Example: Martha has 24-hour accident coverage and is injured in a roller skating accident when she loses control and crashes into a cement wall. While examining and treating Martha for her injuries, the doctors discover that she has a form of cancer.

This policy will provide benefits for the medical treatment of Martha's injuries, and it will even pay disability income benefits if she is unable to work because of those injuries. However, it will not provide any benefits for Martha's cancer treatments or any lost work time due to cancer (because the disease is not work-related).

In yet another approach, 24-hour medical and disability coverage would be provided for all diseases, whether work-related or not, but only work-related accidents would be covered. Here we find broad disease coverage and limited coverage for accidents.

Medical and Disability Package

This coverage package provides the most complete combination of 24-hour occupational and non-occupational coverage. It includes medical and disability coverage for both accidents and diseases on a 24-hour basis (it has been referred to as Universal 24-Hour Coverage for this reason).

In recent years, the National Association of Insurance Commissioners (NAIC) has assisted its membership in the gathering and sharing of information about 24-hour coverage and pilot programs in various states. Key components of this effort included the work done by the NAIC 24-Hour Coverage Working Group and the Workers' Compensation (D) Task Force. The task force identified a number of significant barriers to the implementation of 24-hour coverage. These barriers may be classified as legal, institutional and regulatory. While not attempting a complete discussion of these barriers, we will summarize the nature of these barriers for you.

There are a variety of barriers that have prevented the rapid development and implementation of 24-hour coverage products. There are also some potential conflicts with federal law. There is a need to preserve the "exclusive remedy" aspect of workers' comp benefits. There are institutional barriers due to the different nature of occupational and non-occupational benefits, which entities have traditionally provided them, and how the benefits are usually structured. Additionally, there are a few regulatory issues to be resolved.

Special Exposures

If you are an independent contractor, a subcontractor, an employee of a subcontractor, self-employed, a principal or investor who doesn't earn wages and—in most cases—a volunteer, you will not qualify as an employee under workers' comp.

If this is the case, you might want to secure certificates of workers' comp coverage from the parties with whom you work. Principals may be held liable for the employees of contractors who fail to meet obligations under the law, and contractors can be held liable if their subcontractors fail to meet the obligations.

Summary

Workers' compensation provides medical and disability benefits for occupational injuries or diseases—accidental injuries that occur at work or occupational diseases that are contracted on the job. Workers' comp laws have drastically altered the employee-employer relationship.

This chapter has examined various methods of coverage and health benefits which are available to you as an employee. In the next chapter, we will discuss using other forms of insurance.

Cancer, COBRA, and Other Special Coverages

9

Cancer, COBRA, and Other Special Coverages

In the heated debate between managed care and traditional indemnity insurance, some smaller but equally important health coverage issues are lost. These smaller issues are often related to specialty health insurance policies—matters which are not broad enough to become political debates, but which can be devastating when they impact an individual person or family.

In this chapter, we will consider how some of these smaller coverages work. We'll also take a quick look at the financial and medical factors which impact their coverage.

If insurance companies consider you uninsurable due to your health or medical history, or if you are in the market for more than just your typical medical and hospitalization coverage, consider exploring the options of other, less commonly used forms of health-related benefits or policies.

Some people opt to purchase alternative coverages—on a stand-alone basis or combined with each other—such as dental coverage, vision coverage, a separate prescription plan or even long-term care coverage. Of course, some of these people look for the coverage precisely because they suspect they will have a particular kind of need.

On the other hand, some people choose these coverages for financial reasons: Because their employers offer the insurance for free, or for a discounted fee via a tax-advantaged "cafeteria plan."

Whatever the reason people choose specialty coverages, the plans will likely grow in importance as technology and financial sophistication advance. Some risk experts in the insurance industry predict that soon "health insurance" will be a collection of specialty coverages for specific diseases and conditions. This would allow maximum flexibility for the policyholder—and maximum precision for the insurance company.

In the meantime, specialty coverages remain a specialty. But one that's worth considering in detail.

Cancer Policies

Cancer insurance is sometimes referred to as a limited risk policy or the even older name dread disease policy. The names reflect the basic truth of the coverage: It only provides benefits for a single category of health risks—cancer.

Generally, this type of policy provides a daily benefit or indemnity (such as $50, $75, $100, etc.) if you or a family member is hospitalized for cancer or is receiving regular cancer treatment on either an inpatient or outpatient basis. However, a specific insurance company or particular policy may limit coverage even more steeply. In this case, daily benefits may be provided only for inpatient treatment of cancer with outpatient expenses excluded.

If you have a cancer policy and are hospitalized for cancer-related treatment or surgery, over and above any other benefits, the policy will indemnify you at a specified amount ($100 per day is common) for as long as the treatment or hospital confinement continues. Of course, if you're hospitalized due to a broken leg, the cancer policy will pay nothing.

Cancer policies do contain limitations in terms of both the daily benefit, a policy maximum or a time limitation. For example, a plan may pay $100 per day for up to 30 days of confinement, 90 days of treatment, etc.

A basic medical expense policy or major medical plan will cover cancer like any other illness would be covered—on an expense-incurred basis. The cancer policy indemnifies you on a daily basis without regard to actual expenses incurred.

If you have hospitalization insurance do you need an additional policy for cancer insurance? The answer depends upon your ability to pay extra premium, awareness of the risk of cancer, etc. Because cancer is one of the leading causes of death, most people are aware of its risks and costs. However, this awareness may not create any urgency for "extra protection" by means of a cancer policy.

For example, almost everyone is aware of the relationship between smoking and lung cancer, yet, hundreds of thousands continue to smoke because they don't care or don't believe the cancer will happen to them. Or, even more unfortunately, they simply can't quit.

Do smokers buy cancer insurance? Probably not. Before they issue a policy, most insurance companies that write cancer coverage will ask you if you smoke. If you answer "yes," the premiums are very high.

In most other cases, the premiums for cancer insurance are relatively low—just a few dollars in annual premium per thousand dollars of coverage for a healthy person in his or her thirties.

So, why don't more people buy the insurance? Several reasons stand out. First, many people don't see a reason to buy extra coverage when they already have regular health insurance. Second, most consumers don't like to think about their health in terms of contracting specific, deadly diseases. Third, most insurance companies would rather focus on broad coverages sold to large audiences. They don't encourage their agents to sell specialty policies.

Of course, a particular person may be more aware of cancer's effects, due to his or her own experience—the loss of a loved one to the disease or a family history. This person will probably be more inclined to buy the extra protection.

Buying cancer insurance is a choice you will have to base upon your own specific needs and motivations. The coverage often will duplicate what you are paying for in your comprehensive medical plan. Be sure you understand the limitations and exclusions—whether or not you have any real need for this coverage—before you buy the policy.

Accidental Death and Dismemberment (AD&D)

AD&D is a form of coverage that pays either a specified amount or a multiple of the weekly disability benefit if a policyholder dies, loses his or her sight, or loses two limbs as a result of an accident.

The accidental death benefit—commonly referred to as the principal sum—is actually the "face amount" of the policy. So, if you buy a $100,000 AD&D

> An AD&D plan has two parts: the accidental death benefit and the accidental dismemberment benefit.

benefit, the principal sum paid to your beneficiary if death is caused by an accident is $100,000.

Your insurance company will define—in a liberal or restrictive way—the words *accident* and *accidental death* in the policy.

We will examine the definition of *accident* here, because if you're in the market for health insurance, you probably won't need to determine how your insurance will define *accidental death* for the purposes of receiving health benefits.

If you get in an accident and suffer the loss of a limb—but don't die—the policy's accidental dismemberment benefit will be paid. This benefit is referred to as the capital sum. The capital sum is the same as the face amount. So, if you have a $100,000 AD&D benefit, the capital sum is the same $100,000.

Eligibility for the dismemberment benefit usually requires the actual severance of a body limb such as an arm or a leg.

This is different than loss of use of a limb. And the distinction gets a little gory.

If you are severely injured in an accident and suffer the loss of use of your legs, the capital sum will not be paid for loss of use. Your legs must be severed as a result of the accident.

Most policies will require the severance of two limbs (such as both arms) in order for the full capital sum to be paid. Loss of only one limb frequently results in just 50 percent of the capital sum being paid. AD&D policies usually require that the loss must occur within a specified period of time following the accident, such as 90 days.

For example, if you are injured in an accident and linger between life and death and then finally die four months later, the principal sum would not be paid, since death occurred after the 90-day period.

AD&D benefits are normally purchased in the form of a rider rather than as a separate policy. The premium is characteristically low—often just 10 or 20 cents per thousand dollars of insurance. It would be too expensive for the insurance company to issue a complete policy in return for just a $25 or $50 annual premium. Because of this, the benefits are usually made available as a rider to a life or health policy.

Hospital-Surgery Coverage

This specialty coverage—which was more common in past decades that in the 1990s—insures you against specific, limited costs related to surgical procedures and brief hospital stays.

Most policies may provide first-dollar coverage. That means that there is no deductible, or amount that you have to pay, for a covered medical expense. Other policies may contain a small deductible. In either case, the coverage has to start quickly, because it's designed not to last very long.

Hospital-surgical policies usually do not cover lengthy hospitalizations and costly medical care. In the event that you need these types of services, you may incur large expenses that are difficult to meet unless you have other insurance.

A caveat: These benefits are generally considered to be reimbursements for medical expenses already incurred, and that can raise some tax issues.

You can't deduct medical expenses from your income for tax purposes that have been reimbursed by the insurance company. This is true whether the premiums for the policy were paid by you or your employer.

Catastrophic Medical Coverage

Catastrophic medical coverage pays hospital and medical expenses above a certain—usually high—deductible. You may be responsible for $15,000 or $25,000 in medical bills before a catastrophic policy begins to cover you.

Once you get there, the medical expense benefits usually have no limit—so you are entitled to receive all necessary medical and surgical treatment to cure or relieve a condition. However, your insurance company might set certain maximums or limits for a particular type of care or a particular medical procedure. But, even in this case, overall benefits are usually unlimited.

In many ways, a catastrophic policy will function just like a major medical policy. The policies provide benefits when you have a covered condition that requires hospitalization. These benefits typically include room and board and other hospital services, surgery, physicians' nonsurgical services that are performed in a hospital, expenses for diagnostic x-rays and laboratory tests, and room and board in an extended care facility.

Benefits for hospital room and board may be a per-day dollar amount or part of the hospital's daily rate for a semi-private room. Benefits for surgery typically are listed, showing the maximum benefit for each type of surgical procedure.

Generally, smart consumers use catastrophic policies in one of several ways:

- as additional protection to combine with a limited hospital-surgical policy or a major medical policy with a lower-than-adequate lifetime limit

- as a last-resort policy for people who are in poor health and don't qualify for any other form of coverage

- as back-up coverage for companies that self-fund health insurance benefits offered to their employees or individuals using alternative funding tools like Medical Savings Accounts (MSAs)

Generally, a catastrophic policy is not anyone's first choice for health coverage. Extremely wealthy people may not mind paying a $25,000 deductible out of pocket. People with poor health may have no choice. Otherwise, another form of coverage—even a stingy HMO—will provide more coverage per dollar spent (on premiums and deductibles).

Dental, Vision, and Prescription

In addition to medical and hospitalization coverage, some people opt to buy coverage for things such as dental expenses, vision expenses and even prescription expenses.

Dental insurance—which you can get as additional coverage under most group health plans, through a prepayment plan or through a dental service corporation—will reimburse you for at least part of the money you spend on dental service and supplies.

Dental coverage usually includes payment for preventive care, such as regular checkups, x-rays, and cleanings. It also pays for the things most people hate about dental work: fillings, tooth removal, inlays, bridgework, oral surgery, and root canals. This insurance also will help you in a more limited way—50 percent is a common figure—with expenses for dentures and orthodonture.

Normally, you'll have to shell out a pretty hefty co-payment, although that co-payment may be smaller for preventive services. (Typically, insurance will not help pay for cosmetic work on your teeth.)

Vision plans typically are discount services. For a small fee—about $15 to $20 a year—you get a membership card that entitles you to discounts on eye exams, glasses, and contacts. These discounts (usually in the 50 percent range for eyewear) often are good at a wide variety of stores, including most of the major chains. Some of the plans also offer contact lenses at a discount by mail. Some even provide a discount on non-prescription sunglasses. If you purchase glasses or contact lenses on a regular basis (for example, if you wear disposable lenses), these plans can be cost-effective.

Prescription plans are much like vision plans. They also get you a discount on prescriptions if you visit a participating pharmacy. Again, they typically include most major chains. Discounts range from 5 percent to 50 percent on most drugs. Discounts may be higher if you purchase your prescription drugs through a mail-order program.

Most people who have health insurance do not need a prescription plan—unless they have an extremely high deductible on a major medical plan and purchase prescription drugs on a regular basis.

Long-term Care Insurance

A coverage that has been gaining national attention during the past decade is long-term care insurance. In the late 1980s, the number of companies selling this coverage doubled, according to the Washington Insurance Council. By December 1991, more than two million people were buying long-term care insurance protection.

Long-term care insurance provides a wide array of maintenance and health services—medical care, nursing care, therapy, etc.—if you become chronically ill or disabled and are unable to care for yourself for an extended period of time. It may pay for your care on an inpatient or an outpatient basis—or even entirely at home. These services generally are not covered by other health insurance.

Long-term care can be very expensive. On average, a year in a nursing home costs about $40,000. In some regions, it may cost much more. Home care is less expensive, but it still adds up.

Home care can include part-time skilled nursing care, speech therapy, physical or occupational therapy, home health aides and homemakers. Bringing an aide into your home just three times a week—to help with dressing, bathing, preparing meals, and similar chores—can easily add up to nearly $1,000 a month, or $12,000 a year. Add in the cost of skilled help, such as physical therapy, and your costs could be greater.

Most long-term care policies pay a fixed dollar amount, typically from $40 to more than $200 a day, for each day you receive covered care in a nursing home. The daily benefit for at-home care is usually half the benefit for nursing home care. Because the per-day benefit you buy today may be inadequate to cover higher costs in the future, most policies also offer an inflation adjustment feature.

Unless you have a long-term care policy, you are not covered for long-term care expenses under Medicare and most other types of insurance.

It makes sense for most people with some assets to protect to buy long-term care coverage. Recent changes in federal law may allow you to take certain income tax deductions for some long-term care expenses and insurance premiums.

Limited and Special Risks

Limited risk policies generally include accident-only contracts or contracts that provide coverage for specific situations. For example, a travel accident policy purchased at a local airport usually covers an individual for travel on the airplane on that particular day.

In contrast, a special risk policy is one which covers an unusual type of risk. For example, a professional football player insures his legs so that if he receives a career-ending injury, the policy would indemnify him for the loss (usually loss of income and earning potential). This type of risk cannot be covered under a regular accident policy.

Specified or dread disease policies provide benefits only if you contract the specific disease or group of diseases named in the policy. Because benefits are limited in amount, these policies are not a substitute for broad medical coverage. And specified disease policies are not available in every state.

Hospital Indemnity Plans

In theory, when a person is hospitalized, there are—in addition to medical expenses—additional living expenses incurred. If the hospitalized person turns out to be a homemaker and mother, her family may incur day care and housekeeping expenses while she is in the hospital. And her hospitalization insurance may not cover all of the medical expenses. In short, the woman may well need additional money at the time of a hospitalization.

A hospital indemnity plan provides a daily benefit for each day you are hospitalized as an inpatient—and this is paid without regard to the hospital expenses incurred. This daily amount is paid to you and the benefit is triggered simply by confinement as an inpatient.

An indemnity benefit may be $50, $100, $150, etc., per day. The total benefit due will be a simple total of the number of days you are in the hospital. If you are hospitalized for 10 days and the daily benefit is $100, then you are eligible for a total of $1,000.

Example: Tom has a major medical policy with a $500 deductible and 80 percent to 20 percent co-insurance on the first $5,000 of expenses. He also carries a $100 per day hospital indemnity plan. Tom is hospitalized for major surgery for a total of 20 days. In accordance with his major medical policy, he will have a minimum of $1,500 out-of-pocket expense. If Tom's total expense is $1,500, his hospital indemnity policy will provide him with a check in the amount of $2,000. This check is payable to Tom, not to the provider. Tom can use this amount in any way he pleases.

Generally, hospital indemnity plans are considered to be a supplemental coverage. You can't possibly cover all your hospital expenses with a $100 or even a $200 per day indemnity plan. If you need supplemental benefits— reimbursement for deductibles and co-insurance payments— then a hospital indemnity policy may make sense.

Hospital indemnity policies frequently are available directly from insurance companies by mail as well as through insurance agents. You will find that these policies offer many options on benefits and terms, so be sure to ask questions and find the right plan to meet your needs.

Some policies contain limitations on preexisting medical conditions that you may have before your insurance takes effect. Others contain an elimination period (EP), which means that benefits will not be paid until after you have been hospitalized for a specified number of days. When you apply for the policy, you may be allowed to choose among two or three elimination periods, with different premiums for each. Although you can reduce your premiums by choosing a longer elimination period, you should bear in mind that most patients are hospitalized for relatively brief periods of time.

If you purchase a hospital indemnity policy, review it frequently to check whether you need to increase your daily benefits to keep pace with rising health care costs—or whether your financial circumstances have changed enough that you can drop the coverage completely.

Blanket Health Insurance

Blanket health insurance is primarily an accident-only policy issued to an organization to protect certain groups of people during a particular activity or situation. Blanket policies are commonly provided for schools to cover activities such as athletics, volunteer fire departments or summer camps for small children.

For example, a high school student who is a member of the school's basketball team is probably covered by a blanket health insurance plan. So, if he is injured while engaged in a school activity, expenses will be covered by the blanket health insurance plan. This would also apply to other students involved in various school activities such as cheerleaders, members of other athletic teams, etc. The coverage is designed only to provide protection against injuries incurred while participating in the particular activity.

The policy is issued to the organization and the covered members may receive a certificate of insurance. There may be a premium charged to the individuals. Often, the organization pays the premium—which is modest since benefits are only provided for certain individuals under certain circumstances.

Cafeteria Plans

Congress first authorized so-called cafeteria plans in 1978, as part of the Internal Revenue Code (Section 125).

The term "cafeteria" refers to the way in which you can spend proceeds from the account—on any specific needs which may arise, like choosing dishes in a cafeteria line. Since we're talking about health coverage, this is an unfortunate image. Cafeteria plans are also known as "flexible-spending accounts" and "Section 125 plans."

Any company can set up a cafeteria plan for its employees. This allows the employees to pay for a full menu of medically oriented expenses with pre-tax dollars. This not only reduces taxable income for employees—making the benefits virtually free—it also reduces taxable payroll for the employer.

You can use the money from a cafeteria plan to pay for various deductible expenses. These may include:

- health insurance premiums
- unreimbursed medical expenses (including co-payments for doctor visits or prescription drugs)
- dependent care expenses

- alternative medical treatments (including acupuncture and chiropractic)
- treatment of alcoholism
- programs to lose weight or quit smoking
- vision care (eye doctor visits, glasses, contacts, etc.)
- birth control pills (which some health plans do not ordinarily cover)
- special schooling and care for people with disabilities (from wheelchairs and crutches to artificial limbs and Braille books)
- dental fees, dentures and orthodontia
- psychiatric care
- hearing aids

If your employer offers a cafeteria plan, you choose the amount you would like to have withheld from each paycheck. If you typically spend $200 a month on child care and another $50 on prescription co-payments, for example, you might elect to have $250 a month withheld from your paycheck. If you also have annual expenses for glasses, co-payments for checkups, dental visits and so on, you can have an additional amount deducted each month to cover these costs, as well.

This money is placed into an escrow account. Whenever you have a medical cost that is not covered by your insurance, you submit a claim to the company that manages your employer's cafeteria plan, and that firm debits your account and sends you a check.

A cafeteria plan can be a very good way to save money on health care costs. However, the key is to avoid having too much money deducted from your paychecks. Whatever money you put into a cafeteria plan each year must be used for health care costs. If there is money left over, it cannot be rolled over into the account for the next year or returned to you. As far as you're concerned, it's gone.

Medical Savings Accounts

A new option, when it comes to specialty health insurance, is the tax-free medical savings account (MSA). It combines a long-term savings account and a high-deductible health insurance policy.

As of January 1, 1997, these accounts could be offered to a limited number of individuals who are self-employed or employed at firms with 50 or fewer employees. The accounts are part of a four-year pilot program of a health insurance coverage that was put in motion by the Kassebaum-Kennedy Health Insurance Portability and Accountability Act, passed in 1996. Policies are being sold on a first-come, first-serve basis to those who qualify. The pilot program allows no more than 750,000 policies to be distributed.

How do MSAs work? They're like a combination of a cafeteria contribution plan and an individual retirement account (IRA). You contribute a certain amount of money to the account each month. That money can be used to pay a variety of medical expenses—and it is not subject to income tax.

When you start an MSA, you also switch to a high-deductible catastrophic health insurance policy. (Both are offered in tandem by the same insurance company.) The annual deductible for a single person must be between $1,500 and $2,250. For families, it must be between $3,000 and $4,500.

Individuals then can contribute up to 65 percent of the deductible into the MSA each year. Families can contribute up to 75 percent. The contributions are not subject to federal income taxes and are used to meet the deductible, until the insurance coverage begins to kick in.

MSAs also allow you to use your money for a broader range of services than most health plans. MSAs can cover small, everyday claims, as well as medical expenses that normally would not be covered by other insurance plans— such as dental care, eyeglasses, psychotherapy and home health care. MSAs also can be used toward payment of premiums for long-term care insurance or coverage upon leaving a job.

Money that you put into an MSA grows tax-free, like an IRA or a 401(k) retirement plan. When you turn 59 1/2, the money in the account becomes your property and is no longer restricted to use for health care. Prior to that time, the money can be withdrawn for non-health-related expenses, but you will have to pay ordinary income tax on whatever money you withdraw, plus a 10 to 15 percent penalty.

Premiums for MSAs will differ, depending on such factors as your age, the type of plan, and your place of residence. But if the annual premium is not exhausted at the end of the year, this amount will roll over into the next year.

This is the big difference between an MSA and a flexible-spending health account, which some companies already offer. Flexible-spending health accounts also use pretax dollars for medical expenses not covered by insurance. However, the unused balance in a flexible spending account is forfeited at year end. MSA funds can accumulate over time.

This is why MSA policies are being marketed as investment tools—since the leftover money can be rolled over year after year and collect interest. Leftover money can be used for future health care expenses, or be invested in stocks, bonds and money market accounts.

There are even managed care MSAs. Kentucky-based Humana Inc. offers an MSA program through its wholly-owned subsidiary, Employers Health Insurance Co. Other insurers that are offering MSAs include Blue Cross/Blue Shield, Golden Rule, American Medical Security Group and Fortis.

At the end of the pilot program's term, which is December 31, 2000, Congress will decide whether to keep the MSA program and broaden it, or discontinue it.

If You Leave Your Job

If you have health insurance through your employer and you leave the job—whether you're fired or you quit—the odds are that you will want to keep your coverage for a time.

Under the *Consolidated Omnibus Budget Reconciliation Act*, or COBRA, which is part of a federal law enacted in 1986, you have the right to keep your coverage at group rates if you lose your group health insurance because of a reduction in your hours of employment or because you leave or lose your job—unless, of course, you are fired for gross misconduct. You also have the right to continue coverage for your spouse and any dependents.

COBRA only applies, however, to employers with 20 or more employees, at least half of the time during the preceding year. How long you can keep the coverage depends on your particular qualifying event—that is, dying, being fired, quitting. Different coverage periods follow each of these events.

If you were fired (for anything other than gross misconduct, in which case you don't qualify at all), you, your spouse, and dependent children are entitled to 18 months of continuous coverage.

If your COBRA coverage is about to expire—assuming you haven't taken another job in the interim that provides group health insurance—you can apply to the insurance company for conversion from COBRA to an individual policy. You must do so within 31 days of termination of COBRA. The company is not obligated to provide you with an individual policy, however, if they only sell group insurance.

Your former employer will not keep paying for the health insurance. You'll have to start picking up the tab. The insurance company can charge you 102 percent of what the coverage under the group plan actually costs (the extra 2 percent is an allowance to cover administrative costs). Be assured that, even with the two points, this amount is almost always less than what you would pay if you purchased your own individual coverage—and it is often substantially less.

By law, your employer is required to let you know about COBRA and what steps you must take to retain your health insurance coverage. Your employer also will break down the costs for various coverages you may have, so you can choose to continue all or only some of them. For instance, you may decide to keep your HMO coverage but give up your vision and dental plan.

The Health Insurance Portability and Accountability Act also made a few changes to the provisions of COBRA, which became effective January 1, 1997. Now, newborn and newly adopted children of people who have COBRA coverage automatically qualify for the coverage, as long as you can enroll them within 30 days of the adoption or birth. In addition, a disabled COBRA beneficiary is eligible for 11 additional months of coverage if he or she was determined to have been disabled under Social Security at the time of a qualifying event or at a time during the first 60 days of continuation.(The disabled individual must notify the plan administrator of his or her disability status within 60 days of the determination and within the first 18 months of continuation.)

If your COBRA coverage is about to expire and you anticipate getting another job that provides health insurance soon, you may want to consider a temporary insurance policy.

A temporary medical policy is fairly limited, but it will protect you from catastrophic medical expenses. It usually will have a deductible. After that, it will reimburse you for a percentage of your costs. Some plans will reimburse you on a percentage basis up to a set amount (sometimes $5,000), then pay 100 percent of your costs above that amount. A temporary medical policy will pay typical hospitalization costs—but only for procedures that are medically necessary, at rates that are usual and customary—as well as recovery costs, including time in a nursing home or in-home visits from a registered nurse. It often will not pay for any condition you had during the 24 months prior to the start of the policy, or for any self-inflicted injuries or anything that might be covered by workers' comp insurance.

Also excluded are coverage for injuries incurred in a war (you should be covered by the military, if you're serving), dental treatment, routine physicals and immunizations, routine pediatric care of a newborn child, normal pregnancy or childbirth, sterilization (or the reversal of sterilization), mental illness, alcoholism or drug abuse, prescription drugs and medications that you get when not in a hospital, treatment outside the United States—and the list goes on.

In addition, if you purchase 120 days' worth of temporary medical coverage and get a job in 30 days, the temporary insurance cannot be canceled. (Ordinarily, if you had some other sort of medical insurance, you could get the unused portion that you have paid for refunded.) However, there is probably a probation period with your new employer, during which you are not eligible for the company's medical plan. So, a temporary policy to tide you over for that period may be worth the money.

Summary

If you are buying any kind of specialty health insurance, read and compare the policies you are considering before you buy one, and make sure you understand all of the provisions. Marketing or sales literature is no substitute for the actual policy. Read the policy itself before you buy.

Ask for a summary of each policy's benefits or an outline of coverage. Good agents and good insurance companies want you to know what you are buying. Don't be afraid to ask your benefits manager or insurance agent to explain anything that is unclear.

And bear in mind: In some cases, even after you buy a policy, if you find that it doesn't meet your needs, you may have 30 days to return the policy and get your money back. This is called the free look option. In order to use it effectively, you need to know the right questions to ask.

Choose the Right Plan

Choose the Right Plan

Choosing a health plan is not the easiest task in the world. Or the most enjoyable. But going without health coverage is a bigger risk than most people can afford. What if you get injured and require surgery? The cost of a hospital stay can be as much as $600 a day. What if you or your significant other becomes pregnant? Even through a clinic, the price of prenatal care and delivery can exceed $5,000.

Health coverage is designed to help you in these situations—to assume the risk of paying your medical bills. A good plan provides you with necessary funds to cover hospital and physician expenses associated with a serious illness, thus preserving your savings and other assets. So, it's important that you put some time and effort into deciding which plan is best for you and your family.

Although there is no one "cream of the crop" plan, there are some plans that are better than others for your specific needs. Health plans tend to vary, both in cost and the ability to get the services you need. Although no plan will pay for every health care cost that you may incur, some will cover more than others.

Health insurance plans are usually indemnity (fee-for-service) or managed care. But, as we've discussed earlier, there are other ways to obtain health insurance, including:

- workers' compensation benefits for occupational disabilities
- Social Security disability benefits
- Medicare, if you are eligible
- work-related benefits through employer-sponsored plans
- health coverage under any statutory plans

Any of these programs may offer you enough health coverage so that you would not need to buy standard policies. However, that will usually not be the case.

When considering a health plan, you should try to figure out the total cost to you and your family, especially if someone in your family has a chronic or serious health condition.

Indemnity and managed care plans differ in their choice of providers, out-of-pocket costs for covered services, and how bills are paid. Indemnity offers you more choice of doctors (including specialists, such as cardiologists and surgeons), hospitals, and other healthcare providers than managed care. In addition, indemnity plans pay their share of the cost only after they have received a bill.

Managed care plans usually have agreements with certain doctors and hospitals to provide services at reduced costs. With this type of plan, you will have less paperwork and lower out-of-pocket costs.

Over the past decade, the distinctions between indemnity and managed care have blurred. Indemnity plans offer managed care-type cost controls, and managed care plans allow their members to use providers that are not within the plan's network.

Indemnity Plan

With an indemnity plan, you can use any doctor or hospital you wish. You or they send the bill to your insurance company, which pays part of it. Under most plans, you have to pay a deductible before your insurance company will pay.

Once you meet the deductible, most fee-for-service plans pay a percentage of the usual, customary and reasonable charge (UCR) for a service.

Your insurance company usually pays 80 percent of the cost and you pay the co-payment (co-insurance), or the other 20 percent. If a doctor charges more than the company's UCR rate, you will have to pay the difference.

An indemnity plan typically pays for things like medical tests and prescriptions as well as charges from doctors and hospitals. But, it usually won't pay for preventive care, like annual checkups.

Managed Care Plans

If you decide that an indemnity plan isn't for you, you may want to look into one of three basic types of managed care: PPOs, HMOs and POS plans.

A PPO or Preferred Provider Organization is the closest thing to an indemnity plan. A PPO contracts with doctors, hospitals and other providers who have agreed to accept lower fees for their services. If you choose a doctor within the network, you will pay a lower co-payment. You also may go outside the network if you choose. However, if you do go outside the network, you will have to meet the deductible, and your co-payment will be higher due to higher charges for services outside the network.

HMOs—the oldest form of managed care—offer a wide range of benefits, including preventive care, for a set monthly fee. There are several kinds of HMOs. There are staff or group models in which you visit a plan doctor at central medical offices or clinics. Another type of HMO, an individual practice association (IPA), has network contracts with physician groups or individual doctors who have private offices.

HMOs provide you with a list of doctors from which to choose a primary care doctor, who will coordinate all your medical care. Your primary care doctor will be responsible for referrals to specialists. Some HMOs require you to pay a copayment for each visit. But many HMOs don't require you to pay anything. If you belong to an HMO, it will cover only the costs for doctors in that HMO. If you go to a doctor outside the plan, you could end up footing the bill.

Point-of-Service (POSs) Plans are similar to indemnity plans in that you can still get some coverage if you go outside of the plan. Although a POS requires you to choose a primary care doctor from the plan's network, he or she can make referrals outside of the network, and your plan usually pays all or most of the bill.

In addition, a POS allows you to refer yourself to a provider outside the network and still find some coverage—that is, if you are willing to pay co-insurance.

Group Policies

Many people get their health insurance—indemnity or managed care—as an employee benefit through their job or the job of a family member. Health insurance first became an employee benefit in the U.S. during World War II.

"Many companies found that offering healthcare coverage was an effective way to attract scarce workers without violating the wartime freeze on salaries," said Kathleen Sebelius, insurance commissioner for the state of Kansas. "After the war, full health care coverage soon became an expected benefit of big-business jobs."

You can usually join or change group health plans once a year during open enrollment. But once you make a decision, you have to stay with that plan for at least a year.

Individual Policies

If you are self-employed or if your company does not offer group policies, you can buy individual health insurance. The policies often cost more than group policies—but it's usually better to be safe with coverage than sorry without it. Especially when one major medical expense can make one, two or even 10 years' worth of premiums pay for themselves.

If you belong to a union, professional association, or social or civic group, which usually have health care coverage you could be eligible for health coverage they provide for members.

Medicare and Medicaid

If you are 65 or older, you are probably eligible for coverage under Medicare, the federal health insurance program run by the Health Care Financing Administration. If price is the problem, you might want to look into Medicaid. This type of program provides medical assistance to low-income families (especially families with children and pregnant women), and disabled people. In some cases, if you are covered under Medicaid, you are required to join a managed care plan—so check with your county's Social Services Department to learn more.

Preexisting Conditions

You'll also want to investigate whether or not the plans you are considering at exclude coverage for preexisting conditions. Most insurers would prefer not to pay for treatment for a preexisting condition, such as an ulcer or a gallstone and others will cover the condition, but not until after a waiting period (usually six months to a year).

However, under the Health Insurance Portability and Accountability Act, a preexisting condition is covered without a waiting period when you join a new group plan if you have been insured the previous 12 months.

Your insurance company may also restrict certain benefits for a set period of time. For instance, it may not cover any expenses related to pregnancy until your coverage has been in effect for one year. So, if you or your spouse is planning to become pregnant, you'll want to get your health coverage sorted out as far in advance as possible.

Plan Benefits

What kind of plan is right for you and your family? Only you know for sure. The plan that is "best" for your next door neighbor may not be the "best" plan for you and your family.

In addition to basic benefits, you might want to find out if the health plan you are considering covers:

- physical exams and health screenings
- care by specialists
- hospitalization and emergency care
- prescription drugs
- vision care
- dental services

The Department of Health and Human Services Agency for Health Care Policy and Research (AHCPR) also recommends looking into how a plan handles the following:

- care and counseling for mental health
- services for drug and alcohol abuse
- obstetrical-gynecological care and family planning services
- care for chronic (long-term) diseases, conditions or disabilities
- physical therapy and other rehabilitative care
- home health, nursing home, and hospice care
- chiropractic or alternative health care, such as acupuncture
- experimental treatments

If health education and preventive care benefits are important to you, you might want to ask about services such as, shots for children, breast exams, Pap smears, or programs to help quit smoking.

Making the Right Choice

When comparing coverage, it is vital to look into a plan's limitations, exclusions and reductions to determine which expenses are not covered. For instance, many policies will pay only for treatment that is deemed "medically necessary" to restore you to good health. These policies often will not cover routine physical examinations or plastic surgery for cosmetic purposes. Additionally, some plans limit or won't pay for programs for chronic disease, or various medicines or equipment.

Indemnity and managed care plans typically won't cover treatments that are experimental. In this case, you would want to know how the plan decides what is or is not experimental as well as your options if you disagree with a plan's decision on coverage.

What You Will Pay

As we discussed earlier, your health insurance won't cover you for everything. If you opt for a reimbursement-style program, you'll also have to choose a deductible and at other times you'll have to pay a copayment.

In order to get a true idea of what your costs will be under each plan, you need to look at how much you will pay for your premium and other costs. You can't possibly know what your health care needs for the coming year will be, but you can guess what services you and your family might need.

To figure out what the total costs to you and your family would be for services under each plan, it makes sense to ask the following questions:

- Are there deductibles you pay before the insurance begins to cover your costs?

- After you have met your deductible, what portion of your costs are paid by the plan?

- Does this amount vary by the type of service, doctor or health facility used?

- Are there copayments you must pay for certain services, such as doctor visits?

- If you use doctors outside a plan's network, how much more will you pay?

- If a plan does not cover certain services or care that you think you will need, how much must you pay?

- Are there any limits to how much you must pay in case of major illness?

- Is there a limit on how much the plan will pay for your care in a year or over a lifetime? (A single hospital stay for a serious condition could cost hundreds of thousands of dollars.)

Some people choose a deductible in the thousands of dollars—making theirs, in essence, a catastrophic insurance policy. In this case, you'd absorb all the everyday costs of medical care, from doctors visits to prescriptions. But, if you got seriously ill, you'd be covered. If you are single and healthy, this could wind up saving you money.

For most people, a deductible in the $100 to $250 range is easiest to live with. But look into other deductibles, too. If your family has been healthy for a number of years, you may want to switch to a deductible of $500 or $1,000. You'll notice a sizable reduction in premiums. (Just remember that you'll have to pay your own way until you satisfy the deductible.)

You'll also want to investigate what the insurance company considers usual, reasonable and customary charges, if at all possible. That's because the charges a company considers normal for a particular medical procedure in a specific geographic area are the maximum it will pay. If the charges are higher, you'll be responsible for the difference.

Another way you can save money on your premiums is by paying them annually. It's worth looking into how much the service fee is for monthly payments—and inquiring about a discount for prepayment.

Even if you don't get to choose the health plan yourself (for example, your employer may select the plan for your company), you still need to understand what kind of protection your health plan provides. The more you learn, the more easily you'll be able to decide what fits your personal needs and budget.

Applying For Insurance

To get an accurate quote for health insurance, you will have to fill out an application—completely and correctly. If you lie on the application, the company can not only deny you coverage for a problem down the road, it can rescind the policy entirely. And, most companies can get your medical information anyway through a non-profit association called the Medical Information Bureau (MIB).

The MIB was formed in 1902 by a group of doctors who were also medical directors at several large insurance companies. Because their insurance companies had lost significant dollars to dishonest applicants, they sought a means to centralize health-related information on individual applicants and reduce the potential for fraud.

Before you apply for insurance, it might be a good idea to check if there's a report on file for you—it's at no charge. And, if there is one and it's wrong, you can correct it. Telephone MIB at 1.617.426.3660 and ask for your free report.

The application will ask for your age and health history. In addition, insurance companies often ask your doctor for your medical records, and they may require you to undergo a physical with one of their doctors, or even get additional blood tests. (However, they cannot ask you for an HIV test, unless you are also applying for disability income insurance— and then it has to be with informed consent.)

In completing the application, you will have to let the insurance company know about preexisting conditions—even if you're getting coverage through a new plan at work. The company will want to know what illnesses and health problems you have had during the last couple of years (possibly longer).

Your age is an important factor in pricing and obtaining insurance. Many insurance companies have age bands, when it comes to costs for coverage. For instance, everyone 21 to 25 may fall into one price range. Everyone 26 to 30 would cost a bit more to insure each month. And so on.

Insurance companies prefer to write policies for young, healthy people, and they prefer to stay away from older, less healthy ones. So, it pays to pick a good plan when you're relatively young and stay with it, if you can.

Some companies also allow you to change your mind after you purchase health insurance, but only if the policy has a free look or review period, which typically ranges from 10 to 30 days. So, you'll want to read your policy as soon as you get it.

You may even want to ask your pharmacist and your doctor how different plans are handled before you sign on the dotted line—or sign your check. Your regular providers should be more than happy to tell you which companies and which plans are easy to work with, and which ones make life difficult for providers and patients.

Choosing a Doctor

Whatever type of plan you choose, you will need to select a doctor, whether it's from a network list, a preferred list, or on your own. If you are in a managed care plan, ask your plan for a list or directory of its providers. They may also offer help in choosing a doctor that's right for you.

Once you have the names of doctors who interest you, you should check them out. The AHCPR provides the following list of suggestions:

- Ask plans and medical offices for information on their doctors' training and experience.
- Look up basic information about doctors in the Directory of Medical Specialists, available at your local library. This reference has up-to-date professional and biographic information on about 400,000 practicing physicians.

- Use "AMA Physician Select," which is the American Medical Association's free service on the Internet for information about physicians (http://www.ama-assn.org).

- Find out whether the doctor is board certified. Although all doctors must be licensed to practice medicine, some also are board certified. This means the doctor has completed several years of training in a specialty and passed an exam. Telephone the American Board of Medical Specialties at 1.800.776.2378 for more information.

- Find out if any complaints have been registered or disciplinary actions taken against the doctor. To find out, call your State Medical Licensing Board.

- Find out if any complaints have been registered with your state Department of Insurance. (Not all departments accept complaints.)

- Set up a "get acquainted" appointment with the doctor. Ask what charge there might be for these visits, if any. Such appointments give you a chance to interview the doctors—for example, to find out if they have much experience with any health conditions you may have.

Summary

Choosing the right health coverage comes down to asking a lot of questions. These questions will generally fall into two categories: first, how the plan responds to various medical conditions and needs, and second, what limitations and exclusions the plan uses to control costs. In this chapter, we've offered some of the specific questions to ask.

It can be tough to find someone who will answer these questions at a specific insurance company or HMO. In some cases, you may need to talk to a broker or agent. In others, you may have to spend some time on the telephone finding the right person.

You may not want to do all this research for six or eight different plans—but most insurance decisions boil down to two or three options. If you find yourself wondering whether to choose a flexible managed care plan or a cost-saving indemnity plan, the decision is probably worth an hour or so and a couple of calls.

If you get your health coverage through work, contact your human resources manager. He or she should be able give you information on the coverage and plans available through your employer. Or, you may wish to call the plan directly.

In the end, though, the decision will usually be yours. It's the way that the insurance and health care industries are moving. Self-service coverage means asking questions for yourself.

Filing a Claim

Filing a Claim

All the work you put into choosing the right kind of health insurance for you and your family comes to a point when you make a claim. Getting the best health care means understanding how your health plan works, what your rights are, and how to complain if you need to.

It's important to remember that this is a process. Making a claim is like any other aspect of a contract transaction. The best companies will be supportive and understanding of what you've experienced. But what you really want is to have your claim paid. This chapter will show you how you can make a claim in the most effective way.

When you do have to make a claim, don't be afraid to count on your agent—if you have one. Agents who are eager to keep your business can become your best advocates.

Although state laws vary on requiring consumers to make claims within a certain time period, most insurance companies prefer that claims be filed within 15 days, or as soon as reasonably possible. If someone's been hurt in an accident, there's been serious damage or some law has been broken, call the police first. Then call your insurance company.

Your insurance company may grant you a little extra time if, for example, you're seriously injured and notice cannot be given within the listed time period. You can usually do this by calling the insurance company directly, through your lawyer or through your insurance agent.

Of course, insurance companies want to be notified as quickly as possible. And it's true that, the sooner you file a claim, the sooner you'll get a settlement. After the insurance company receives notice of your claim, it will usually furnish claims forms within a specified number of days.

"Once something happens, you need to let us know immediately, because we may need to investigate something, like tire tracks for example, which don't stay around very long," says one spokeswoman for State Farm Insurance Companies. "Know who you were in an accident with. Get the other party's insurance information, the number on the police report and the name of the person who's insured before calling us."

Most states require insurance companies to either process a claim, or at least tell you why it hasn't been processed, within 60 or 90 days. If it fails to do so, you may submit a written proof of the occurrence, character and extent of the loss either in the form of an official accident report or an affidavit.

If the company does send you the claims forms you can fill out a proof of loss and submit it within 90 days of the covered loss to be reimbursed. Once again, extra time is granted if it's not possible for you to respond within this time limit. But don't go over one year unless you're legally incapacitated because you may lose your opportunity to collect on a claim. Issues of incapacitation are less important than your forgetfulness and inaccuracy.

· An important note: Remember to include all the associated expenses too. Most disputes over claims forms involve situations in which policyholders only include a portion of the expenses they've accrued. Then, when the insurance company only covers some of the bills, accusations start to fly.

Getting Your Claim Paid

Benefits are payable directly to you. Generally, medical insurance policies provide reimbursement for covered expenses. This means your insurance company wants you to pay your medical bills first, and then it will pay you. Traditional insurance companies would rather not get involved with doctors or hospitals at all.

Whether the benefits go to the estate or to an incapacitated person, the insurance company has the option of paying benefits of up to $1,000 to any relative who appears to be entitled to receive the funds.

> In the event of your death, the benefits may be paid to your estate.

Since your health insurance policy is a legal contract, the insurance company is obligated to pay the described benefits for all covered expenses under the policy. If your insurer doesn't live up to it's obligations, you have the right to sue them. However, no legal action may be taken against the company prior to 60 days after proof of loss has been furnished, or more than three years after the date proof of loss is required to be furnished.

For example, you submit proof of loss for hospital bills. The insurance company doesn't deny the claim, but it doesn't pay it either. You get on with your life and four years pass before you realize the insurance company never reimbursed you. At this point, you can't sue the insurance company because you've forfeited the right of legal action by taking too long.

While your claim is being verified, your insurance company also has the right—at its own expense, of course—to require you to submit to a physical examination. However, this typically occurs only in rare cases in which an insurance company suspects fraud.

One common error that can slow down the claims process is a misstated age on your insurance application. If this occurs, any benefits payable will be adjusted to the amount that the premium would have been, if purchased at the correct age. This item usually governs situations in which older policyholders lie about their age in order to get cheaper premiums.

Delaying Payment

Insurance companies used to settle claims more quickly than they do today. The theory was that if they settled quickly, they could do so for a smaller amount—they'd just make sure the policyholder signed a release denying any further claims related to the accident in question. But, policies have become more complicated and many insurance companies have changed their tactics. Now, many insurance companies delay payments as long as they can without inviting lawsuits.

You don't have to accept the delays, though. There are several basic principles that you should use in collecting from insurance companies:

- Analyze every part of loss for how it might be covered by your policy.
- Consider all of the claims you might make following an accident or loss. If you have health insurance or are covered under workers' comp can you make claims under these coverages?

Don't accept a first offer—or even a first denial—by an insurance company as the final, unequivocal word.

Insurance companies will delay or deny claims if they can. If they do, ask for an explanation for their delay or denial. In response, you should gather facts and reread your policies yourself. If you can't decipher everything in the policy, talk to your agent or—if necessary—a lawyer.

You might check the policy's exclusions too. Exclusions identify types of losses that are not covered by the policy. They help to shape the coverage or narrow the scope of coverage by specifying the losses that the policy won't pay for.

Exclusions usually form the basis of most of the legal disputes that occur between policyholders and insurance companies. They are generally included to accomplish these four broad purposes:

- to clarify intent of coverage
- to remove coverages for losses which should be covered by other insurance
- to remove coverage for losses which result from above-average risk factors which are not anticipated in rates and premiums (usually this coverage is available at an additional charge)
- to remove coverage for catastrophic losses which are generally not insurable (although coverage may be available through special insurance pools or government programs)

Even if denial isn't your insurance company's ultimate goal, by playing the denial game, it can achieve something almost as advantageous—a lengthy delay in paying the claim. The longer an insurance company can hold on to its money, the better off it is. But the law, and more importantly the courts, don't give insurance companies free rein to delay fair settlements as they please.

What To Do if the Company Denies a Claim

If your insurance company denies your claim, ask why the claim was rejected. If the company's answer involves a service that isn't covered under your policy (and you're more than certain it is covered), check the claim form. It could be that the provider entered an incorrect diagnosis or procedure code. You might also want to check whether your deductible was correctly calculated or whether you didn't skip an essential part of the process. If everything still seems to be in order, you can then ask your insurance company to review the claim.

For cases like these, it often helps to keep written records of the following:

- All correspondence with the plan.
- Claims forms and copies of bills.
- Phone conversations—the date and time, the people you speak with, and the nature of each call.

If the insurance company still denies your claim or insists you take it to court for your money, don't be intimidated. Ask for the language in your policy or in state law that allows it to deny your claim. Save all paperwork and log all phone conversations with company representatives.

If what your insurance company says doesn't agree with your reading of your policy, ask your state regulator. While state insurance commissioners usually have no legal authority to force an insurance company to pay an individual claim, the commissioner can fine a company or take other punitive actions if an insurance company makes a practice of unfairly underpaying or denying claims.

Most health plans have some sort of appeals process that you and your doctor may use if you disagree with the health plan's decisions. If your plan refuses to provide or pay for services, you can complain or file a grievance about any decision you feel is unfair—or you may appeal it.

Bad Faith

Lawsuits or regulatory complaints relating to delays or denials usually allege bad faith on the part of the insurance company. This is one of the heaviest clubs a policyholder can wield to strike back at an insurance company.

One way in which an insurance company can act in bad faith is by not investigating a claim with an eye toward providing coverage.

"The investigation should be geared toward paying the claim, not denial. Nine out of 10 times, however, that investigation is designed to turn something up that justifies denying the claim. Their eye should be toward protecting their policyholder, but it's not," said William Shernoff of Shernoff, Bidart & Darras, a California-based risk management consulting group.

Regulatory Reform Issues

In 1993, California Insurance Commissioner John Garamendi put in place a number of regulations to simplify the claims process. The California regulations were loosely patterned after model standards adopted in 1991 by the National Association of Insurance Commissioners. Insurance industry analysts predicted their use in California may influence other states' treatment of similar standards.

Among Garamendi's 1993 regulations:

- Within 15 days of any notice of claim, an insurance company must acknowledge receiving the notice. The company must also start its investigation within 15 days of receiving a notice of claim.

- Within 40 days of receiving a notice of claim, an insurance company must affirm or deny the claim and affirm or deny liability.

- If 40 days isn't sufficient time, the company must write to the claimant and specify why more time is needed, and what further information it needs.

- A denial of a claim, in whole or part, must be accompanied by a letter that spells out the policy provisions and factors upon which the company is relying. All denials must include a notice that the company's decision can be reviewed by the Insurance Department.

- Insurance companies must disclose to their policyholders all benefits, coverage, time limits or other relevant provisions of any policy they have issued that may apply to a claim.

- Any other communication that "reasonably suggests that a response is expected," with regard to a claim not in litigation, must be responded to within 15 days of receipt.

Outpatient Services

If you have coverage for outpatient services under your plan, the plan will usually pay for 80 percent of covered outpatient services and supplies, subject to the maximum benefit amount shown in your policy's benefit schedule. You will be required to pay the other 20 percent of the charges or co-payment.

Here's a list of outpatient services and supplies that health plans typically cover:

- x-ray and fluoroscopic examinations
- radium, and other radioactive substance
- electrocardiograms, microscopic, and laboratory tests
- drugs and medicines which may be purchased only on the attending physician's written prescription and which are dispensed by a licensed pharmacist
- casts, splints, braces, crutches and artificial limbs
- oxygen and equipment used for its administration

Outpatient services are covered only when rendered due to injury or sickness, while coverage is in force for the insured person, and at the direction of a physician or surgeon. These outpatient benefits do not include benefits for the services of a radiologist, pathologist, anesthesiologist, physician or surgeon.

Inpatient Care

Hospital inpatient care provides you with benefits for charges a hospital makes on its own behalf. For example, room and board, nursing care, etc. Most plans limit room and board to a semi-private room rate, a maximum dollar amount per day, and a maximum number of days confinement. Benefits for miscellaneous services are also limited to a maximum dollar amount.

For example, you have inpatient coverage with benefits of $300 a day for a maximum of 365 days. You're confined for 10 days in a private room. The hospital charges $325 a day for a private room and only $250 a day for a semi-private room. Your policy will only pay $2,500—the semi-private room rate for 10 days. You must pay the difference.

Inpatient benefits can provide coverage for confinement for mental, emotional, or nervous disorders, alcoholism and drug dependency—but not more than 30 days in any one policy year.

Confinement means that a policyholder is confined in a hospital or mental hospital for 24 hours or more and a daily charge is made. In order for a period of confinement to be covered, it must occur because of injury or sickness, begin while coverage is in force, and at the direction of a physician or surgeon.

Also, you might want to check with your plan administrator to see if your policy covers extended care facility coverage, or extra hospital miscellaneous expense coverage. These coverages are optional and provide an additional amount of insurance while you are an inpatient. Hospital intensive care unit coverage may also be covered.

The term "one period of confinement" is important because basic hospital expense policies usually limit the maximum benefit for each period of confinement to a number of days and a total dollar amount. In addition to a continuous period of confinement, multiple confinements due to related causes and separated by less than 180 days will be treated as a single confinement.

For example, you have an appendectomy and spend three days in a hospital. After release, the incisions become infected and you're readmitted 20 days later. For benefit purposes, both periods in the hospital related to the appendectomy are treated as a single confinement.

Who is Covered Under The Policy?

In the general agreement of your policy, the insurance company states that it relied upon the information given in the application and issued the policy because you paid the first premium. This is important because coverage applies only to each person shown in the policy schedule (which may be cross-referenced by page number). After the policy is in effect, any changes you make to the persons insured under the policy, coverages, or benefits must be attached to the policy and coverage will remain in force for any period in which the insurance company accepts a premium payment.

Paying Your Premium

Your first premium payment usually will be due in advance. Although the policy says that subsequent premium payments are also due in advance, you're usually allotted a grace period of 31 days after the premium due date. You can pay your premiums annually or, if acceptable to your insurance company, semi-monthly, quarterly or monthly. If you do not pay your premium on time, the insurance company may deny coverage.

Your insurance company has the right to raise your premium on each annual anniversary date to reflect the advancing age of the insured persons under your policy, increased costs of medical care, and any changes in deductibles (higher deductibles tend to reduce the premium, while lower deductibles tend to increase the premium).

If you move to a new residence, a premium adjustment may be made to reflect the premium rates that apply to the new location.

Excluding the above premium changes, your insurance company may change premiums only if it does so for all policies of the same type in your state. It can't change the premium for an individual policy except for changes in age, medical cost, deductibles and location.

Termination of a Policy

Your insurance company can terminate your health insurance coverage if you fail to pay a premium before the end of a grace period. It won't affect any claims that you incurred before your coverage ended, but it will terminate your coverage on the original due date of your premium. Any claims that you make during the grace period will not be covered.

For example, you failed to pay your premium due February 15. On March 15, your coverage terminated for nonpayment of premium. You were hospitalized in January, submitted a timely notice of claim, and furnished proof of loss on April 1 (within the 90-day requirement). The claim for the hospital expenses is covered.

How Individuals are Terminated

In some policies, your insurance may be continued only until you reach age 65—or become eligible for Medicare—whichever occurs first. Coverage will end during the month of the event on the day that coincides with the policy date. For instance, your 65th birthday occurs on August 20 and you become eligible for Medicare on September 10. Even though your policy date is January 15, your coverage ends on August 15 (the day that matches the policy date during the month of your birthday). If you have children, their coverage usually ends when they reach age 25 (though some policies will use other ages), get married or are no longer dependent on you for coverage.

Coverage for a child will not end if you have a child that is mentally or physically handicapped, remains dependent on you, and is not eligible for Medicare. But you will have to show proof of incapacity and dependency within 31 days of the child's 25th birthday in order to receive coverage. The insurance company may require you to submit additional proof, but not more than once each year after the child reaches the age 27.

Whenever a policy is terminated due to the above factors, coverage usually will continue for any period in which a premium has been accepted and claims for expenses incurred prior to termination will still be covered.

Extension of Coverage

As mentioned earlier, your insurance company will usually extend your coverage if you are being treated for a continuous injury or sickness if the policy is not renewed or if coverage terminates for a reason other than nonpayment of premium. Coverage is typically extended up to 90 days.

Another option when coverage terminates due to age or eligibility for Medicare, is to convert to another policy. You have to apply for a converted policy and your insurance company will only issue this type of policy after it receives a written application and payment of the first premium at least 31 days before coverage terminates.

Preexisting Conditions

As we have mentioned throughout the book, preexisting conditions are an important issue to look into when shopping for health insurance. Why? Limits on preexisting conditions are usually the most common issue in health insurance coverage disputes.

Most plans don't cover preexisting conditions during the six months following the effective date of coverage, or any disease or physical condition named or specifically described as excluded in any endorsement attached to this policy.

Pay close attention to any talk of specific or custom exclusions on any policy. This holds especially true if you've had any notable illness or disability in the last ten years—even if it's healed or in remission.

An example: When you applied for insurance, you disclosed that you'd been treated for a heart condition during the past two years. If the insurance company doesn't attach a specific exclusion, you would have coverage for the heart condition—but only after a waiting period. If the heart condition is excluded, you will never have coverage for that condition, regardless of how long the policy is in effect. While some states are moving toward cost containment, others have moved in the opposite direction—stressing what they call "consumer choice."

Adding Insureds to a Policy

If you're about to have a baby, you might want to read your policy carefully and be extremely cautious about changing your insurance.

Under some plans, a new child will be automatically covered for 31 days after the date of birth. However, in order for coverage to continue beyond that time, you must notify the insurance company to request coverage and pay an additional premium for the child within the 31-day period.

Coverage for a newborn child includes coverage for:

- congenital defects
- birth abnormalities
- injury or sickness

An important note: No benefits are provided for premature birth (where no defects or abnormalities are involved) or well-baby care.

If you want to add someone other than a newborn, such as, a new spouse, or adopted child, you must make an application for coverage, submit proof of insurability, and pay an additional premium.

Summary

When it comes to insurance, problems don't surface until you make a claim which is denied or underpaid. Many of the same issues that influence how much a health coverage plan costs also influence how the same plan pays claims.

The main mistake people make when they have trouble getting a claim paid is that they assume the insurance company or managed care group has more authority than it really does. Insurance companies don't have any special power over policyholders—both sides are simply parties to a contract.

That contract—the insurance policy—states how many issues will be resolved. Claims disputes are certainly one of those issues. But, within the parameters set by the contract, there is much room for negotiation and compromise. Much of the time, the insurance company or managed care group is counting on that room to work to its advantage. After all, it employs people who spend their days reading and enforcing insurance contracts.

But there's room in the contract for you, the policyholder, too. If you don't like the fact—or the manner in which—a claim was denied, you can press your issue. Your pressure will usually need to start within the insurance company's own appeals process. If that doesn't accomplish anything, you can resort to regulatory agencies.

The important thing to remember is that insurance companies are in business to make a profit. This will usually give them—despite how their employees may act—an impulse to settle disputes that they can't avoid. If your position is well-reasoned and consistently made, you may get more satisfaction than you initially expected.

Tips For Smart Shoppers

Tips For Smart Shoppers

Once upon a time, people could go to any doctor they wanted. If their general practitioner decided they needed to see a specialist, they could see any specialist they pleased. If they needed medicine, they could go to any pharmacy and get exactly what the doctor ordered.

But things have changed. Today, we have a lot more choices, including HMOs, PPOs, generic drugs, lists of doctors we can and can't see, treatments we are allowed—only after two or three doctors agree that it's necessary.

The changes are due, in part, to skyrocketing medical costs. In fact, according to the Washington Insurance Council, in 1969 per capita expenditures for health care were about $268 per year in the United States. By 1990, that figure jumped to nearly $2,567. During the same 20-year period, health expenditures grew from 5.3 percent of the gross national product (GNP) to 12.2 percent.

Health insurers have had to absorb some of these costs—and they've had to contend with ever-increasing fees for doctors, lab tests, prescription drugs, and hospitals. On the other hand, they have passed many of the increased costs on to you—the consumer—in the form of higher premiums. But there comes a time in every industry's lifecycle when it can't pass the costs on any longer and it has to do something else. It has to cut costs.

Still, you do have choices when it comes to your health insurance—whether you are buying your own coverage or getting it through your employer.

Getting The Most Out of Your Health Plan

In order to get the most out of your health plan, you should stay informed. How? Read your health insurance policy and/or plan member handbook thoroughly, making sure that you understand the sections that pertain to the benefits, coverage, and limits provided under the policy.

Some companies allow you to change your mind and get your money back after you purchase health insurance—but only if the policy has a "free look" period, which typically ranges from 10 to 30 days. So, read your policy as soon as you get it.

Insurance consumers—like consumers of anything—should compare the various products they are considering buying. The problem with insurance is that, people don't always know where to look.

You should have enough insurance to cover you and your family against the most serious and financially disastrous losses that can result from an illness or accident. If you are offered health benefits at work, carefully review what each plan offers to make sure the one you select fits your needs. If you purchase individual coverage, buy a policy that will cover your major medical expenses and pay them to the highest maximum level.

Call the health plan. Most offer brochures on the various coverages, as well as the information that you should and need to know. Additionally, they may offer telephone numbers for hotlines, services, etc. which might also be useful in your search for the "best" plan for you.

You might also want to speak with the Human Resources director or health benefits officer at your workplace to learn more about your policy. They can usually provide you with some information, brochures, and personal insight as well as provide you with key contact numbers for your plan.

Comparing Plans

Most people tend to choose between a traditional indemnity plan and a managed care plan. As with any plan, whether you end up choosing a fee-for-service plan or a form of managed care, you must examine a benefits summary or an outline of coverage. The benefits summary gives you a description of policy benefits, exclusions and provisions which makes it easier to compare policies.

Read the summaries carefully. Think about you and your family's specific health care needs. You may not want coverage for pregnancy, but you may want coverage for chiropractic services.

Here's a list of important questions to ask:

- What exactly does the plan cover? Some services such as mental health, drug rehabilitation or dental care, may not be included at all. While you can't possibly predict all of your health care needs, find out if the treatments that you need are covered. Also, find out if treatments that are considered experimental or non-traditional are permissible and, if you're interested, if alternative or holistic treatments are covered.

- What will it really cost? Don't just look at the monthly premiums. Consider the overall costs, including co-payments and deductibles. Some plans offer a reasonable limit on the total you will pay each year. Others place a lifetime limit on what the company will pay, which you can reach if you have one major health problem.

- Do you have a choice of doctors? Be sure to have some flexibility. Also be sure at least a few local hospitals and pharmacies are covered under the plan.

- Is there a utilization review? In some plans, you cannot switch doctors or see a specialist without authorization. What happens if you don't like the doctor you choose?

- Who decides what is considered medically necessary? Does the insurance company or the doctor decide?

- What about preexisting conditions? If you have a pre-existing condition, such as high blood pressure, you may be liable for all costs relating to the illness. Know when and if your insurance pays for any illnesses you may have.

- What is the relationship between your doctor and your health insurance company? If your doctor receives a set fee per patient (capitation) or receives a bonus for minimizing costs (incentives), your healthcare could get shortchanged. A doctor may be reluctant to order tests or referrals under these situations.

> Gag clauses can prevent doctors from revealing their compensation or discussing treatment options not covered by the plan.

- Does the plan you're considering have a grievance procedure? What if something goes wrong? Can you appeal? Be sure to talk with someone who is authorized to answer your questions, like the plan administrator, and keep good records. Who regulates HMOs in your state and what's the procedure to lodge a complaint if you think you're being treated unfairly?

When comparing coverage, it is critical to look into a plan's limitations and exclusions to determine which expenses are not covered and which are restricted. For instance, many policies will pay only for treatment that is deemed "medically necessary" to restore you to good health. These policies often will not cover routine physical examinations, cosmetic procedures or even the costs of eyeglasses or hearing aids.

The following is a list of services you might want to ask about when looking into a plan:

- covered medical services
- inpatient hospital services
- outpatient surgery
- physician visits (in the hospital)
- office visits
- skilled nursing care
- medical tests and x-rays
- prescription drugs
- mental health care
- drug and alcohol abuse treatment
- home health care visits
- rehabilitation facility care
- physical therapy
- speech therapy
- hospice care
- maternity care
- chiropractic care
- preventive care and checkups
- well-baby care
- dental care
- other covered services

Old Fashioned vs. New-fangled

Is access to preventive care and routine check-ups an important factor in your choice of a health plan? If you answered "yes," you might want to go with a traditional indemnity-type plan. But, if you'd rather save money on premiums, an HMO might be a smart choice.

A traditional indemnity plan or fee-for-service coverage gives you freedom of choice. You choose the doctor you want to see and then pay a fee for each service rendered. If the services are covered under your policy, your insurance company will reimburse you for some—but not all—of the cost. Many policies pay 80 percent of the costs. Fee-for-service plans cost considerably more than managed care plans.

However, if you want lower premiums, you will have to give up some of this freedom of choice (unless of course, your doctor is part of the HMO network and listed as your primary physician). Rather than being penalized by getting less of a reimbursement, as in a PPO plan—which gives you some choice—with an HMO you'd have to pay the whole bill yourself. (Clearly, this is a strong incentive to see only providers within the HMO.)

Today, many HMOs have added options to their plans which allow you to see a doctor of your choice who is out of network. Of course, this, too, will cost considerably more than a co-payment.

A PPO or POS combines the features of fee-for-service plans and HMOs. These types of managed care plans provide a choice regarding doctors, hospital, etc. whereas an HMO restricts choice to a network provider. Under these plans you will also get some reimbursement for covered services from a provider. The only major difference between a PPO and a POS plan is that under a POS plan, a primary care physician coordinates your care, and in most cases, PPOs do not.

If your doctor is already a contracting provider with a PPO or HMO, you may be able to save some money by going with one of the more restrictive plans—and you'd still get to see the doctor of your choice. In other words, read the preferred provider list, or the HMO's provider list, before you decide.

HMOs can be quite restrictive, and many people don't learn the details of their plans until they have a medical problem— or a problem with coverage. Critics question whether managed care has been stretching its method of cost containment too far. Among other things, managed care is criticized for depleting funds for scientists and medical schools, proposing gag rules to restrict treatment discussions between doctors and patients, and offering financial incentives to its staff for curtailing medical costs.

It's worth looking into how much the service fee is for monthly payments—and inquiring about a discount for prepayment. Even if you already have health insurance, you'll want to review your policy once a year to be sure it still matches your needs. As the health care system continues to change, your health insurance should change with it.

Insurance Companies, etc.

Most life and health insurance companies market both group and individual hospitalization coverage. There are also service organizations, such as Blue Cross/Blue Shield, that provide prepaid medical and health benefits in accordance with state laws that recognize them as not-for-profit organizations and exempt from state premium taxation.

The only difference between the two is that commercial insurers have a contractual relationship with you, and service organizations have a contractual relationship with providers. With a service organization, you use the services of the contracted doctors or hospitals—participating providers— and claims are settled directly with the providers.

Cancer and Other Coverages

If you want a little more coverage than a standard policy offers, you can purchase—as a stand-alone policy or combined coverage—a number of alternative coverages to fill in the gaps in traditional health insurance. Accidental Death & Dismemberment riders cover you for the severance of arms, legs, or the loss of vision as a result of an injury or accident.

Individual dental expense benefits—typically not provided by insurance companies—can be purchased separately for preventative maintenance (cleanings and x-rays), repair (fillings, root canals, etc.) and replacement of teeth.

If you or someone in your family has a chronic disease or disability, you might want to purchase long-term care insurance to cover a wide range of care services, including nursing home care, home-based care, and respite care.

There are also a variety of special insurance policies that provide a limited amount of coverage—including, travel accident insurance, specified disease or dread disease insurance, hospital income insurance, accident-only insurance, blanket insurance, etc.

One optional coverage that may be worth the money is prescription medication coverage. This type of coverage will cover the costs of medication required, in lieu of a stated cost—usually two, three, or five dollars.

Government Plans

There are two main programs in which the government becomes a health care provider: Medicare and Medicaid.

If you are age 65 or older—or disabled—you could be eligible for Medicare, a federal health care program financed by the Social Security taxes that are taken out of you and your employer's paychecks.

The other major federal health care program is Medicaid. Qualification for benefits in a Medicaid program are based on financial need and the coverage offered under the plan is fairly limited.

Individual vs. Group Policy

Health coverage is usually available on an individual or group basis. Group coverage—typically what most people have—is somewhat cheaper than individual coverage.

You can get group coverage through your employer, but unions, professional associations, and other organizations also offer the coverage.

Your employer may choose to assume some or all of the costs of your premium—usually lower due to lower administration costs for large groups—or he could choose to deduct it from your pay.

To save even a little more money, your employer might want to set aside a sum of money in a secured account to pay for your health care costs when they arise. This type of plan is referred to as a self-funded plan.

Deductibles

As with other types of insurance, the higher your deductible, the lower your premium. For most people, a deductible in the $100 to $250 range is the most manageable. But compare other deductibles, too. If your family has been healthy for a number of years, you may want to switch to a deductible of $500 or $1,000. You'll notice a sizable reduction in premiums.

Save money on premiums, if necessary, by taking larger deductibles and covering smaller costs yourself.

Most policies have an out-of-pocket maximum—when your covered expenses reach a specified limit in a given policy year, a reasonable fee for the benefits that are covered under your plan will be paid in full by your insurer, and you no longer have to pay the co-insurance. However, if your doctor bills you more than the reasonable and customary charge, you may still be required to pay some of the costs.

Most policies have lifetime limits, too. It's smart to look for a plan with a lifetime limit of at least $1 million. If it's lower than this, you could run through coverage if you ended up having major health problems for several years.

Other Issues

Insurance agents and companies may not claim that they represent the Medicare program, the Social Security Administration, or any government agency. They may not imply that the policy they are selling is guaranteed, approved or otherwise backed up by the government. If someone calls you claiming to have been authorized by the government to review your existing insurance program, don't agree to an appointment.

Anyone who tells you that he or she is a counselor or adviser for any association of senior citizens, may in fact just be a licensed insurance agent trying to sell you a Medicare supplement insurance policy. Ask for credentials, the licenses they hold, and what kinds of products they are authorized to sell. A business card is not a license.

Never let an agent talk you into signing any form, application, or document in blank. When you are buying a policy, never pay your policy premium in cash or make out a check to the agent's personal account. The agent should make it clear that you have the option of paying your premiums directly to the insurance company.

You may want to check with your state insurance department to see if there have been a lot of complaints about the insurance companies you're considering. There are agents and companies whose lack of professionalism and ethics can cost consumers dearly. But there are also ways for you to protect yourself. Knowledge is power, and being aware of your coverages as well as your legal rights and responsibilities will help you avoid being taken advantage of when choosing a plan.

Life Insurance Made E-Z

Life Insurance is the most common investment consumers make, However, most people buy life insurance without understanding how it works. Insurance companies are eliminating and selling coverage directly to consumers. Consumers now need to make life insurance decisions for themselves. *Life Insurance Made E-Z* helps make these decisions.

Essential subjects in the book:

Stock No.: G349
$14.95 6" x 9"
232 pages Soft cover

- Why you need life insurance
- The general rules of life insurance
- Different types of coverage
- Who's involved in a life insurance contract
- Insurable interest
- The life insurance application
- Benefits of life insurance
- Considering other sources of protection
- Planning money for the long term
- Future college costs
- Naming and maintaining beneficiaries
- Exclusions and limitations
- Special family needs
- Using life insurance for medical treatment
- . . . and much more.

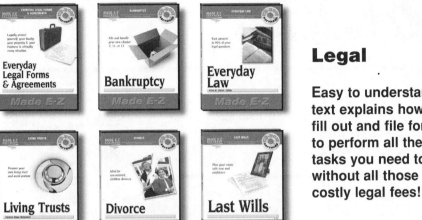
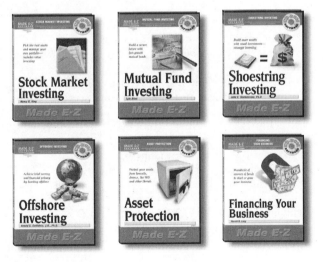

By the book...

ss 2001.r3

MADE E·Z® LIBRARY

Credit Repair — Made E-Z

Buying & Selling a Business — Made E-Z

Bankruptcy — Made E-Z

MADE E-Z BOOKS

Each comprehensive book contains all the information you need to master one of dozens of topics, plus sample forms (if applicable).

Most books also include an appendix of valuable resources, a handy glossary, and the valuable 14-page supplement "How to Save on Attorney Fees."

	ITEM #	QTY.	PRICE‡	EXTENSION
MADE E-Z SOFTWARE				
E-Z Construction Estimator	SS4300		$29.95	
E-Z Contractors' Forms	SS4301		$24.95	
Contractors' Business Builder Bundle	CD325		$59.95	
Asset Protection	SS4304		$24.95	
Corporate Records	SS4305		$24.95	
Vital Records	SS4306		$24.95	
Personnel Forms	HR453		$24.95	
Accounting	SS4308		$24.95	
Limited Liability Companies (LLC)	SS4309		$24.95	
Partnerships	SS4310		$24.95	
Solving IRS Problems	SS4311		$24.95	
Winning In Small Claims Court	SS4312		$24.95	
Collecting Unpaid Bills	SS4313		$24.95	
Selling On The Web (E-Commerce)	SS4314		$24.95	
Your Profitable Home Business	SS4315		$24.95	
E-Z Business Lawyer Library	SS4318		$49.95	
E-Z Estate Planner	SS4319		$49.95	
E-Z Personal Lawyer Library	SS4320		$49.95	
Payroll	SS4321		$24.95	
Personal Legal Forms and Agreements	SS4322		$24.95	
Business Legal Forms and Agreements	SS4323		$24.95	
Employee Policies and Manuals	SS4324		$24.95	
Incorporation	SS4333		$24.95	
Last Wills	SS4327		$24.95	
Business Startups	SS4332		$24.95	
Credit Repair	SW2211		$24.95	
Business Forms	SW2223		$24.95	
Buying and Selling A Business	SW2242		$24.95	
Marketing Your Small Business	SW2245		$24.95	
Get Out Of Debt	SW2246		$24.95	
Winning Business Plans	SW2247		$24.95	
Successful Resumes	SW2248		$24.95	
Solving Business Problems	SW 2249		$24.95	
Profitable Mail Order	SW2250		$24.95	
Deluxe Business Forms	SW2251		$49.95	
E-Z Small Business Library	SW2252		$49.95	
Paint & Construction Estimator	SW2253		$19.95	
MADE E-Z BOOKS				
Bankruptcy	G300		$24.95	
Incorporation	G301		$24.95	
Divorce	G302		$24.95	
Credit Repair	G303		$14.95	
Living Trusts	G305		$24.95	
Living Wills	G306		$24.95	
Last Will & Testament	G307		$24.95	
Buying/Selling Your Home	G311		$14.95	
Employment Law	G312		$14.95	
Collecting Child Support	G315		$14.95	
Limited Liability Companies	G316		$24.95	
Partnerships	G318		$24.95	
Solving IRS Problems	G319		$14.95	
Asset Protection	G320		$14.95	
Buying/Selling A Business	G321		$14.95	
Financing Your Business	G322		$14.95	
Profitable Mail Order	G323		$14.95	
Selling On The Web (E-Commerce)	G324		$14.95	
SBA Loans	G325		$14.95	
Solving Business Problems	G326		$14.95	
Advertising Your Business	G327		$14.95	
Rapid Reading	G328		$14.95	
Everyday Math	G329		$14.95	
Shoestring Investing	G330		$14.95	
Stock Market Investing	G331		$14.95	
Fund Raising	G332		$14.95	
Money For College	G334		$14.95	
Marketing Your Small Business	G335		$14.95	

‡ *Prices are for a single item, and are subject to change without notice.*

TO PLACE AN ORDER:

1. **Duplicate this order form.**
2. **Complete your order and mail or fax to:**

Made E-Z Products

384 S. Military Trail Deerfield Beach, FL 33442

www.MadeE-Z.com

Telephone:
954-480-8933

Toll Free:
800-822-4566

Fax:
954-480-8906

continued on next page

	ITEM #	QTY.	PRICE‡	EXTENSION
Owning A No-Cash-Down Business	G336		$14.95	
Offshore Investing	G337		$14.95	
Multi-level Marketing	G338		$14.95	
Free Legal Help	G339		$14.95	
Get Out Of Debt	G340		$14.95	
Winning Business Plans	G342		$14.95	
Mutual Fund Investing	G343		$14.95	
Business Startups	G344		$14.95	
Successful Resumes	G346		$14.95	
Free Stuff For Everyone	G347		$14.95	
On-Line Business Resources	G348		$14.95	
Life Insurance	G349		$14.95	
Health Insurance	G350		$14.95	
Successful Selling	G351		$14.95	
Everyday Legal Forms & Agreements	BK407		$24.95	
Personnel Forms	BK408		$24.95	
Collecting Unpaid Bills	BK409		$24.95	
Corporate Records	BK410		$24.95	
Everyday Law	BK411		$24.95	
Vital Records	BK412		$24.95	
Business Forms	BK414		$24.95	

MADE E-Z KITS

	ITEM #	QTY.	PRICE‡	EXTENSION
Bankruptcy Kit	K300		$24.95	
Incorporation Kit	K301		$24.95	
Divorce Kit	K302		$24.95	
Credit Repair Kit	K303		$24.95	
Living Trust Kit	K305		$24.95	
Living Will Kit	K306		$24.95	
Last Will & Testament Kit	K307		$19.95	
Buying and Selling Your Home Kit	K311		$24.95	
Business Startups Kit	K320		$24.95	
Small Business/Home Business Kit	K321		$24.95	

MISC. PRODUCTS

	ITEM #	QTY.	PRICE‡	EXTENSION
☆ Federal Labor Law Poster	LP001		$5.99	
☆ State Specific Labor Law Poster (see state listings below)			$29.95	
E-Z Legal Will Pac	WP250		$9.95	

State	Item#	QTY	State	Item#	QTY	State	Item#	QTY
AL	83801		KY	83817		ND	83834	
AK	83802		LA	83818		OH	83835	
AZ	83803		ME	83819		OK	83836	
AR	83804		MD	83820		OR	83837	
CA	83805		MA	83821		PA	83838	
CO	83806		MI	83822		RI	83839	
CT	83807		MN	83823		SC	83840	
DE	83808		MS	83824		S. Dakota not available		
DC	83848		MO	83825		TN	83842	
FL	83809		MT	83826		TX	83843	
GA	83810		NE	83827		UT	83844	
HI	83811		NV	83828		VT	83845	
ID	83812		NH	83829		VA	83846	
IL	83813		NJ	83830		WA	83847	
IN	83814		NM	83831		WV	83849	
IO	83815		NY	83832		WI	83850	
KS	83816		NC	83833		WY	83851	

ORDER TOTAL ☆ Required by Federal & State Laws $

SHIPPING & HANDLING
$4.95 for first item, $1.50 for each additional item
(All orders shipped Ground unless otherwise specified) $

SUBTOTAL $

Florida Residents add 6% sales tax $

TOTAL $

SS 2001 r4

Prices are for a single item, and are subject to change without notice.

MADE E-Z PRODUCTS

PLEASE COMPLETE THE FOLLOWING INFORMATION:

NAME: _____

COMPANY: _____

ADDRESS: _____

CITY: _____

STATE: _____ ZIP: _____

PHONE: ( ) _____

PAYMENT METHOD:

☐ Charge my credit card:

  ☐ MasterCard

  ☐ VISA

  ☐ American Express

ACCOUNT NO.

EXP DATE

SIGNATURE (required for credit card purchases)

☐ Check enclosed, payable to:

Made E-Z Products
384 S. Military Trail
Deerfield Beach, FL 33442

Company Purchase Orders Are
Welcome With Approved Credit

Index